Riding TANDEM

LEANING into the LEADING of GOD

for girls

Tween and Teen Girls
Middle School – High School

Annie Pajcic

THOUARTEXALTED, INC

Creating Art through God's Word

www.thouartexalted.com

RIDING TANDEM FOR GIRLS • Leaning into the Leading of God
Copyright © 2017 by Annie Pajcic
All rights reserved.

ISBN-13: 978-0-9896141-6-0

Art Direction, Interior Composition, and Design by Annie Pajcic
Published by Annie Pajcic Design, Jacksonville, Florida
www.thouartexalted.com

TABLE OF CONTENTS

Leader and Participant's Guide 4
Introduction 5

WEEKS OF STUDY

• WEEK 1:
Time for Takeoff   6
Prayer Requests   10
Journal   11
ART PROJECT: Tires on Fire   17

• WEEK 2:
Time for Takeoff II   18
Prayer Requests   22
Journal   23
MEMORY CARDS   28

• WEEK 3:
Alignment   30
Prayer Requests   34
Journal   35

• WEEK 4:
Alignment II   40
Prayer Requests   44
Journal   45
ART PROJECT: Esther's Spa Treatment 49

• WEEK 5:
Necessary Stops   50
Prayer Requests   54
Journal   55

• WEEK 6:
Necessary Stops II   59
Prayer Requests   65
Journal   66
ART/SERVICE PROJECT: Fleece Blanket 71

• WEEK 7:
Don't Stop Pedaling   72
Prayer Requests   76
Journal   77
MEMORY CARDS   82

• WEEK 8:
Don't Stop Pedaling II   84
Prayer Requests   88
Journal   89
ART/SERVICE PROJECT: Sole Hope   93

• WEEK 9:
Enjoy the Ride   94
Prayer Requests   98
Journal   99

• WEEK 10:
Enjoy the Ride II   106
Prayer Requests   111
Journal   112
MEMORY CARDS   117

• WEEK 11:
Mark the Moments   118
Prayer Requests   123
Journal   124
MEMORY CARDS   129

• WEEK 12:
Mark the Moments II   130
Prayer Requests   135
Journal   136
ART PROJECT: Riding Tandem Journal 144

Notes, About the Author 145
More About ThouArtExalted 146

Let me begin by saying THANK YOU for purchasing Riding Tandem for GIRLS and being a part of our study together!

Riding Tandem for GIRLS is a 12-week Bible study filled with art, fun, and surprises recommended for middle school—high school girls. Riding Tandem follows the acronym **T-A-N-D-E-M.**—T-ime for Takeoff. A-lignment. N-ecessary Stops. D-on't Stop Pedaling. E-njoy the Ride. M-ark the Moments. Each lesson begins with **Ice Breaker Questions** and is followed by a review time for **Journal Questions.** Next, you will dive into the main lesson, **It's Time to Ride** and close with **Prayer Requests. Journal Questions** are included after each lesson intended for girls to develop a deeper one-on-one relationship with Jesus. And of course, there is a FUN surprise—either an art project, recipe, memory cards, or service idea following most chapters. I believe the purpose of a small group is to have fellowship with one another, laugh, and grow in the knowledge of God's Word. After leading small groups for years, here are some TIPS:

1. Keep track of TIME.

Decide ahead of time how long your group sessions will be. Begin with the ice breaker and journal questions then study the group lesson together. Leave time if you choose to participate in the art project, recipe, memory cards, or service idea. Remember to always look at your watch and keep the conversation going. If you have time at the end, you can always go back to look at a question. Close with taking prayer requests.

2. Keep conversation on TOPIC.

Girls can be easily distracted and quickly get off course. Your job is to keep everyone on track. Ask the Holy Spirit to give you gentleness as you steer the conversation back on topic.

3. Keep TALKY people to a minimum.

Not everyone wants to share in a small group. Try to allow a chance for girls to participate and be careful that no one person dominates the conversation. Be sensitive to the needs of others and ask God for wisdom.

4. Allow TIME to prepare.

As a leader, be prepared to facilitate your small group. You can't lead if you haven't taken time to sit with the Lord and study Riding Tandem.

5. TAKE time to PRAY with and for your small group.

This is one of the most important aspects of your group. I would encourage you to take prayer requests at the end of each discussion time and emphasize the confidentiality of the group. Prayers and discussions are personal and should not be taken outside your small group.

This is not a complete list of "how-to" lead a small group by any means, but hopefully it hit on a few good points! Remember to be real. Be yourself. Be inviting. Allow the Holy Spirit to lead you as you have the privilege to lead your small group. And, if you ever have any questions, please e-mail me at apajcic@thouartexalted.com.

We are praying for you!

Have you ever ridden a tandem bicycle?

Growing up, our family had a tan and white striped Schwinn Tandem. Oh, the beauty of a bicycle built for two! Yet because our family was built for six, seats were limited. At the age of seven I could barely reach the pedals AND hold on to the handle bars at the same time. If by chance I did get to score a seat (on the back), I would find myself lowering my body just enough to reach the pedals. I found out early on that it was easier to let one of my sisters take the front seat and do **all** the work. I was along for the ride and glad for it.

Honestly, my family had good reason not to trust my biking abilities. While I would not describe Jacksonville as a "hilly" town, there is one place where you can feel the slight downhill tilt of the road. The combination of this hill, a parked car, my distraction, and the front end of my banana seat bicycle was not good. BOOM. You can only imagine.

Fortunately, **Riding Tandem** is not about how many accidents we have had. It is not about climbing the ranks of the seating chart, reaching for the pedals, or navigating parked cars. **Riding Tandem** is about an authentic, everyday, one-on-one relationship with God. It's about learning our position on the back of the bike and trusting God with the front steering. Our personal relationship with God is built for two. He is the Captain, so we must learn to lean into His leading, pedal forward, and trust Him with the directions. **Riding Tandem** will teach us that while our final destination is heaven, our destiny on earth has purpose. We are not just along for the ride. We are **a part** of the ride. God wants us to live an abundant life completely surrendered to His leading. **Riding Tandem** with Jesus is letting go of the handlebars and experiencing His power as we pedal. Everyday.

Where is God taking you today? Are you equipped for the ride? He promises never to leave your side as the Captain of your life. Do you trust His leading? Are you willing to let go of the handlebars? Allow me to pray this prayer as we begin the journey of **Riding Tandem.**

*Dear Lord, today I choose to hop on the back seat of the tandem. I choose to let You steer the story of my life and teach me the lessons ahead. Life is Your classroom, and I am Your student. I will take the time to sit, listen, study hard, and do my work. I will pedal hard and learn to trust in Your teaching. While I can't see the road ahead, You can. I know that You go before me. You are my lead. You are my guide. I know there will be times when I am afraid and want to clutch on to my handlebars and take control. Please remind me that You are right there with me. You will never leave me. At times, I might want You to speed things up, and at other times, slow life down. Remind me that Your timing and pace are perfect. We are in this ride **together**. With You as my Captain, I can press on, be patient, and persevere with joy. Climb on sweet Lord! Balance the bike for me so I can take the position as Your co-captain. Lead me in the way everlasting so that I may soar in Your presence. It's time to ride. Amen.*

It's a beautiful day for a bike ride!
Lots of love and grace,

Annie

ICE BREAKER Questions

I break for ICE BREAKERS

1. What do you remember about your FIRST bike? What color was it? Did you have a basket? If so, what did you carry in it?

2. When did you first learn how to ride a bike? Do you have a funny story to tell?

IT's TIME TO RIDE: Group Lesson

Imagine a tandem bicycle has just arrived at your back door. Immediately you notice the note tied to the front handlebar.

Welcome! Let Me introduce myself. My name is Captain, and I am overjoyed that you chose Me to ride with you through life. We are going to take amazing adventures together. As your Captain, I know the direction we will be taking. There's no need to be distracted by all the latest gadgets and gizmos because I have all the equipment you will need. I have plenty of water and be assured, the rest stops are well planned in advance. If you ever feel tired, insecure, or winded, just stop pedaling and coast. I have you in the palm of My hand. If you ever get scared, worried, or doubt My leading, just lean in and trust that I am steering you in the right direction. Make sure to mark the special moments we will have together and always remember to enjoy the ride. Life can get tricky sometimes, but if you trust Me, I will give you eyes to see from My perspective—the right perspective. Do not worry. As your Captain, I am in full control. Before you climb aboard, please read My instructions and know your seating assignment. It is very important to know our takeoff procedures before we ride together on this tandem bicycle.

With everlasting love,
Your Captain

It's **T-ime for Takeoff.** For the next twelve weeks, our transportation of choice is the tandem bicycle, and **Riding Tandem** begins with being confident of **takeoff procedures.** As we take a closer look at takeoff protocol, we will become more familiar with who our Captain is and how our choice in seating position prepares us for our day.

The tandem bicycle will be our visual focus for **Riding Tandem.** Take a look at this illustration and soak in the imagery.

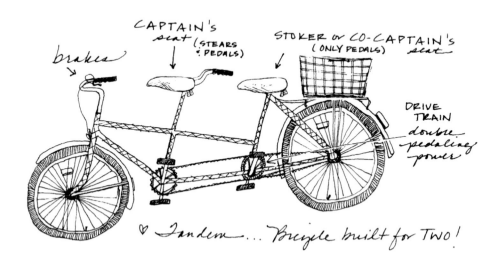

CAPTAIN's
seat (STEARS & PEDALS)

STOKER or CO-CAPTAIN's
(ONLY PEDALS) seat

brakes

DRIVE TRAIN
double pedaling power

♥ Tandem... Bicycle built for Two!

T-ime for Takeoff begins with **seating positions.** It is very clear this bicycle is built for **two.** The front rider is called the captain while the back rider is called the co-captain or stoker. The captain's job is to steer the bike **and** pedal. The co-captain is **only** to pedal. Carefully look at the words AND and ONLY.

```
Why do AND and ONLY make a difference in seating
positions? In your life, who do you see on the front and
back seat? Where do you prefer to ride?
```

_____

_____

_____

Look up the following verses and write ways Jesus would make the BEST Captain.

   • **Philippians 2:9-11**

_____

_____

_____

• **John 14:6**

_____

_____

• **John 13:12-17**

_____

_____

_____

• **Colossians 1:15-20**

_____

_____

_____

We can see with clarity that Jesus is best suited for the job as our front seat driver. Our Captain is the Lord Jesus. Every knee will bow one day to recognize this powerful truth. He is the way, the truth, and the life. He is our Teacher. He is Lord. His name alone is a title of honor, respect, and reverence. He is also a humble servant. He is the image of the invisible God, and **all** of God's fullness dwells in Him. He is the Creator and Sustainer. He is the beginning of all things, holds everything together, and made peace for all things through his blood shed on the cross (Colossians 1:15-20).

Now that we have established who the Captain is, where is our seating position on the tandem bike? You guessed it. On the back.

It is important to note again that the back rider, called the co-captain or stoker, **only** pedals. We are not called to steer. I know this is tough news for some of us, or maybe all of us. It's not easy hopping on the back. Why? We want to be in charge. We want the control seat where we can make the calls and call the shots. But in God's economy, this is **not** our position. Our position is on the back.

Look up the following verses and take note of the repeating word that prepares us to be co-captains and stokers with Jesus as our Captain. What is God's response when we take this position?

Repeating Word/ God's Response

• **1 Peter 5:5-7**

_____/_____

_____

_____

- **Psalm 25:9**

_____/_____

_____

- **Matthew 23:12**

_____/_____

_____

Humility. When we are humble enough to move to the rear, God guides and teaches us what is **right**. When we clothe ourselves in humility, God responds with **grace**. When we humble ourselves, God **lifts us up**. Humility is the opposite of pride. The position of pride wants the power and prestige of the Captain's seat. But God's Word makes it clear that "pride goes before destruction" (Proverbs 16:18). Humility will always instruct us how to lean into the Captain's leading. No more backseat driving, girls. Keep pedaling and **leave the steering to God**.

```
Where in your life is it hard to give up control and
humbly trust God with the front seat? Write down your
answer and share with your group if you feel comfortable.
```

_____

_____

_____

_____

_____

Below, write a prayer to your Captain. How are you going to hop on the back and trust Him to lead?

> Dear Captain,
>
>
>
>
>
>
>
>
>
>
>   With love,

I RIDE
for PRAYER
REQUESTS

1. Look up and write down 2 Timothy 1:6-7.

* What are some specific gifts God has given you?

2. Read 2 Timothy 1:6-7 in your Bible and in the margin.

> "And that special gift you received. . . keep that ablaze! God doesn't want us to be shy with his gifts, but bold and loving and sensible."
>
> 2 TIMOTHY 1:6-7 (ICB)

* The translation from the International Children's Bible of 2 Timothy 1:7 reminds us to keep the special gifts of ministry that God has given us ablaze!

Paul is reminding young Timothy, and us, to stir up or fan into flames the gifts God has given. Did you notice that the co-captain is also called a "stoker?" A stoker was in charge of fueling a furnace. As we learn our position on the back, **as stokers**, we are in charge of *tending the furnace* that generates **power** for us to pedal. This power comes not from pride or our own personal efforts to pedal, but from our **humility** as we learn to trust in the Lord. Tending the furnace is taking the time to spend with God, building a one-on-one relationship, spreading His Word, and serving Him with our gifts. This is preparation for **T-ime for Takeoff** at its core.

* How are you going to "tend the furnace" and spend time with God serving Him with your gifts?

3. Read Jeremiah 17:7-8.

* What happens when you place your trust in the Captain?

* What are your fears?

* What are your worries?

* Did you know the Bible calls you a tree? When your confidence is in the Captain, your tree will always bear fruit. The fruit you produce are the gifts you are fanning into flames for God! What kind of tree are you? What kind of fruit are you producing. Why?

4. Read Psalm 9:10. What do you think it means to KNOW Jesus?

"Those who know the Lord trust him. He will not leave those who come to him."

PSALM 9:10
(ICB)

* Why can you place your trust in the Captain?

* The word for "not leave" can also be translated never forsaken or never leave. How does this give you comfort when you are going through a difficult situation?

5. Read Matthew 16:13-17. What is the first question Jesus asks the disciples?

* What is Peter's response?

* Who revealed this mystery to Peter?

6. Read Romans 10:9-10.

* What two things are needed to believe in Jesus according to Romans 10:9-10?

"If you declare with your mouth, "Jesus is Lord," and if you believe in your heart that God raised Jesus from death, then you will be saved. We believe with our hearts, and so we are made right with God. And we declare with our mouths to say that we believe, and so we are saved."

ROMANS 10:9-10
(ICB)

* Have you ever made a declaration that Jesus is Lord? What is the promise when you believe that Jesus is the Captain of your life? Write down when you first believed and give a shout out to your Captain!

What a great week! Let's close in prayer:

Dear Lord, thank You that You are my Captain. I pray that I would continue to fan into flames the gifts You have given me to glorify Christ. Help me dig my roots deep and be confident that YOU are leading me! You have my life on a perfect path, a perfect timeline, and going the perfect speed. Thank You for steering me and allowing me to pedal forward. I believe in You and love you. Amen.

TIRES on Fire!

Art Supplies:

- Hula Hoop
- Elmers Glue
- Glue Gun (Optional)
- Colored Fabric
- Scissors
- Old Color T-shirts
- Wooden Clothes Pins
- Scrapbook Paper

Art Instructions:

1. Take your fabric and cut 8 strips measuring 2 inches x 3 feet. (Tip: I like to tear my fabric.)

2. Take your first strip and tie it onto your hula hoop. Start wrapping your fabric around the hoop leaving about 5 inches to tie to the next strip of fabric. Add a little Elmer's glue (or hot glue) to keep fabric in place. Keep wrapping until your entire hoop is covered in fabric.

3. Take an old T-shirt and starting at the bottom, cut strips of fabric about 1.5 wide. Cut through front and back so you will end up with a circle of fabric.

Art Supplies

4. Stretch the fabric around your hula hoop and pulling to make the T-shirt as tight as you can, make a knot at end to secure.

5. For your final touch, cover some clothes pins with scrapbook paper and clip pictures, notes, Scriptures, and more onto your TIRE on FIRE. Hang in your room to remind you to FAN INTO FLAMES the gifts that God has given to you!

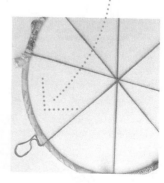

Week TWO: TIME FOR TAKE-OFF (part 2)

I break for ICE BREAKERS

1. Do you have a rare talent you can share with the group? Hint: Maybe you have a double jointed finger or can wiggle your ears.

2. What is the bravest thing you have ever done?

JOURNAL review

STOP and take five to ten minutes to discuss your journal time. How did these Scriptures help you to ride tandem with God this week?

IT's TIME TO RIDE: Group Lesson

T-ime for Takeoff is about developing a personal relationship with our Captain.

As girls with busy lives, and I am sure you have one, we need to make TIME to grow **deeper** in our relationship with the Lord. But how do we do this? As BUSYNESS tends to drive our lives, we need an authentic connection with our Captain. I believe our first step towards building a deeper relationship with Jesus is **knowing** who He is and **why** we believe in Him. We need to be 100% confident in His position as our Captain.

We have learned our position on the back seat and the truth that knowing Him personally opens the door to confident belief and trust. Today, we will look at why it's important to prepare our hearts **before** we ride with God through our day. **We need eyes to see and ears to hear in order to lean into His leading.** We must prepare our hearts by addressing Him with reverence every morning.

Slowly read Isaiah 50:4 in the margin. Why should we spend time with God every morning?

_____

_____

_____

_____

According to Isaiah 50:4, when we acknowledge that our Captain is Sovereign Lord, we are given words to say that **strengthen the weary**. We are also given an **eager** alarm clock to wake us up morning by morning with a listening ear and teachable heart.

Does this describe your relationship with God?

What can you do to make time in your day to spend with the Lord? What words do you need to hear to encourage those around you? Who will you encourage today?

_____

_____

_____

_____

T-ime for Takeoff takes action. It's the daily morning by morning discipline of getting up and sitting with the Lord. I am not talking about casually communicating with our Captain on an every-now-and-then basis but really **knowing Him** on a deeper level, like a best friend. We can't expect the blessing unless we are willing to build the relationship. We need the ears to hear and the hearts ready to be taught. We don't want to miss Jesus in the morning. If we do, we might miss telling about Him during the day.

Read the following verses about Jesus waking up to spend time with His Captain. What were the results of His prayers?

• **Mark 1:35-39**

_____

_____

• **Luke 4:42-44**

_____

_____

I love this exercise! Jesus never slept in! He was disciplined in His T-IME for Takeoff. Notice what happened after His time of prayer. **He was eager and inspired to preach and spread the good news!** When we, too, take the time to spend our mornings with Jesus, our ears are opened to hear the Word. Our lips become a source for healing, and our hearts are open to go and preach the good news of the Kingdom of God. Amen!

God is going to teach us, inspire us, and lead us, but we have to be **still** enough to listen. We have to have teachable and eager hearts to learn. If we are going to have a one-on-one personal relationship with our Captain, the best preparation for the ride is to get to **KNOW Him**.

`Let's make it our goal to wake up morning by morning, read the Word of God, and sit so we can soar into our day. Think of it like riding a bike with no hands!`

`Ah, the freedom.`

I drove by a sign last night that said, "What you look at is not necessarily what you see." Think about this for a minute. Time spent with our Master in the morning is **essential** to our takeoff preparation for the day. It's essential because our **first glance** at something might not be what God wants us to see. Sometimes to really see something, we have to spend T-I-M-E looking at it.

Read Psalm 119:18. Why does God want to open our eyes? What does He want us to see?

_____

_____

_____

_____

`Psalm 119:18` emphasizes that God wants to open our eyes because He wants to show us the **wonderful truths** about Him. The word for wonderful means: marvelous, wonderful, be beyond's one power, be difficult to do.[1] This is amazing! When we take time to spend with God morning by morning, He gives us eyes to see things which only He can accomplish in our lives. We are seeing from a new perspective. His perspective. A godly perspective. Our Captain, the Sovereign Lord, has lots to teach us when we wake up morning by morning. Wipe out the sleepy seeds and **set the alarm.** No snoozing allowed!

`Today, we are going to answer another question:`
`Where is God leading us anyway?`

_____

_____

_____

While we may not always see it, we must **remember** that we are asking God to OPEN our eyes to see the wonderful truths in His instructions.

Look up the following verses and write down where God is leading. What is our role? I'll start us off.

• **Read Psalm 27:11**

God is leading us on a straight path. The New Living Translation says that God is leading (us) along the path of honesty. Our part is to have a **teachable heart** and **follow God's leading.** Honesty is always the best policy even when it's easier to cover up the truth. This verse also reveals that there are enemies waiting for Christians to fall. Follow God's lead and you will not stumble. Now it's your turn!

Where is God leading?/ What is our Role?

• **Psalm 23:1-4**

_____/_____
_____/_____
_____/_____

• **Psalm 139:23-24**

_____/_____
_____/_____
_____/_____

God leads. Our job is to ask, to call, to cry, to remember, to search, and to try. **This is our part.** We have to do our work. We cannot expect God to wave a wand and place us on the yellow brick road. Life is certain to have its share of lions, tigers, and bears. But we have a guide, a teacher, and a loving Father who will protect us along the way. When our hearts grow faint, He is there. When we are overwhelmed, He will lead us to the rock of safety. When we are anxious, He will **lead us.** **He is our Captain.**

Great job today! In closing, write a prayer to your Captain. Tell Him what you would like to learn from Riding Tandem as you ride into eternity together. Try not to clutch on to the handlebars too tightly. Let go and learn to lean into His leading.

_____
_____
_____
_____
_____

I RIDE
for PRAYER
REQUESTS

1. Look up and write down Ecclesiastes 3:11.

* What has been PLANTED in your heart?

* What do you think this verse means?

2. Look up and write down John 3:16.

* What is the same word that you saw in Ecclesiastes 3:11? Why do you think this is significant?

Yes! **Eternity.** Last time I looked, that meant **forever.** Just as an acorn has the DNA to grow into a beautiful oak tree, we, too, have eternity planted in our hearts. Whether we acknowledge it or not, there is an emptiness in us that ONLY God can fill. We long for this relationship. Notice Scripture does not say that God has planted power, position, and prosperity in our hearts. No. Our Creator, who made us His masterpiece, has planted **eternity** into our hearts. The seed of everlasting life is planted in our souls. Belief in Jesus activates the seed and inflames the passion to stoke the fire within us. Life here and now will never satisfy our deep inner longings because we were not made to live on a temporal earth. We were made to live in an eternal heaven.

3. What are some of the things we place in our hearts instead of God to bring us satisfaction?

* Will they completely satisfy you? Why not?

4. What do you think ETERNAL LIFE looks like?

5. What can you learn about Eternal Life from these verses?

   * John 17:1-5

   * What is significant about John 17:3 and KNOWING Jesus? What have we learned this week about getting to KNOW Him?

   * John 5:24

* Romans 6:22-23

* Matthew 6:19-21. What is the difference between an earthly treasure and a heavenly one?

Eternal life is given to all who hear God's Word, believe in Jesus, and **know Him** as their Sovereign Lord. Confession in Christ, the Son of the Living God, saves us from death and ushers us into a life forever in the presence of a Holy God. When we ask God to be our leader, our Captain, He is leading us in lessons that not only prepare us for today, but prepare us for the ride tomorrow—and forever. **Everlasting life.** This is why our decisions for today are so important. Our opportunities for today can and will affect our tomorrow. Our choices for today have future implications. Our prayers for today have lasting effects for years to come. Are you getting this picture? God is preparing us for **eternity** while He is preparing us for **today.**

Matthew 6:19-21 calls us to store up treasures in heaven. What is the difference between an earthly treasure and a heavenly one? I am quite confident God is not talking about how many friends follow you on Instagram, how athletic you are, your latest haircut, and if you have a Snapchat account. God treasures open hearts and open hands. When we follow Him to serve the poor, help those in need, give up worry, smile with thankful hearts, obey His teachings, live with humility, love unconditionally, hope expectantly, and believe confidently . . . we are storing up treasures in heaven! If we are leaning into the leading of God and allowing Him to steer our tandem bike into everlasting life, then we are storing up treasures in heaven.

Eternity is our final destination.

To get to KNOW Jesus, we MUST KNOW His Word! Color copy these verses and place them in your room, on your locker at school, or in your backpack. Find a friend and challenge each other to memorize them! (Ask your leader to provide a FUN SURPRISE if you memorize all FIVE!)

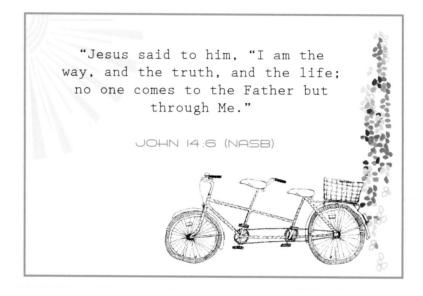

"Jesus said to him, "I am the way, and the truth, and the life; no one comes to the Father but through Me."

JOHN 14:6 (NASB)

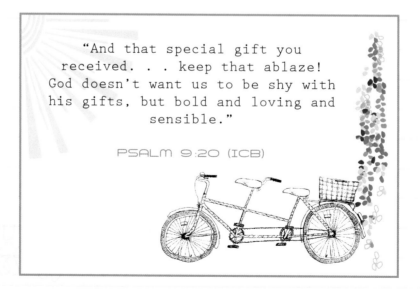

"And that special gift you received. . . keep that ablaze! God doesn't want us to be shy with his gifts, but bold and loving and sensible."

PSALM 9:20 (ICB)

"Humble yourselves, therefore, under God's mighty hand, that he may lift you up in due time. Cast all your anxiety on him because he cares for you."

I PETER 5:6-7 (NIV)

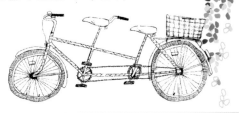

"The Sovereign Lord has taught me what to say, so that I can strengthen the weary. Every morning he makes me eager to hear what he is going to teach me."

ISAIAH 50:4 (GW)

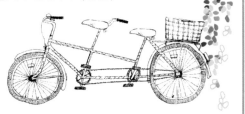

"Open my eyes that I may see wonderful things in your law."

PSALM 119:18 (NIV)

Week THREE: ALIGNMENT

I break for ICE BREAKERS

1. What was the worst thing you ever had to wear to school?

2. Have you ever broken a bone? Did they have to put it back into alignment?

JOURNAL review

STOP and take five to ten minutes to discuss your journal time. How did these Scriptures help you to ride tandem with God this week?

Before we begin week two, let's take time to review.

T-ime for Takeoff prepares us to ride with God in this tandem adventure called life. God is our Captain who steers, pedals, and leads our days. We are the co-captains and stokers that pedal to receive the power. **The tandem bike was built for two just like our relationship with God.** We have to know our Captain personally to believe with confidence and trust in His leading. Spending time with Him morning by morning opens our eyes to see and ears to hear His wonderful truths. God leads us along straight paths and ultimately into eternity. What a week. There is so much more to learn!

IT's TIME TO RIDE: Group Lesson

This week, we come to the letter "A" in our T. A. N. D. E. M. acronym, which represents A-lignment.

A-lignment is essential when Riding Tandem. Why? When we are not aligned, we will fall off the bike. Plain and simple. In bicycle terms, this action is called **tandem toppling** (for real!). The Captain has to steady the bike before the co-captain can hop on. When there is no Captain to balance the bike, the co-captain will topple.

What great imagery! We, too, will fall when we do not allow our Captain to steady our lives. When we can barely open our eyes, God is waiting for us to wake up so He can steady the bike for our journey ahead. Look at the synonyms for the word **steady.** Which one listed below best describes God to you? Circle your answer.

> "Be strong and courageous; don't be terrified or afraid of them. For it is the LORD your God who goes with you; He will not leave you or forsake you."
>
> DEUTERONOMY 31:6 (HCSB)

Steady: immovable, never failing, solid as a rock, steadfast, durable, constant, reliable, safe, unchangeable.

I liked **durable.** This makes me think of the Duracell® battery. They last the longest and have extra-staying power. Duracell® promises that "their batteries will hold out the longest, by supplying power long after their competitor's batteries have died out." [2]

God, like Duracell®, has durability.

What does Deuteronomy 31:6 say about God's staying power?

_____

God is always reliable, and He promises never to leave us, especially when we are afraid. He is our Captain and will steady the bike for us, everyday, before we hit the day running (or biking).

Pick a few of the following verses to look up and discuss why you think God's durable qualities help us avoid tandem toppling?

- **Psalm 111:7**

_____
_____

- **Hebrews 6: 17**

_____
_____

- **Hebrews 13:8**

_____
_____

- **1 John 1:5**

_____
_____

- **John 14:6**

_____

_____

- **John 1:1**

"In the beginning was the Word, and the Word was with God, and the Word was God." John 1:1

_____

_____

- **Matthew 5:48**

_____

_____

God is not only durable, He is also faithful and trustworthy. **God is unchangeable.** He is the same yesterday, today, and tomorrow. He is the way, the truth, the life, and in Him there is no darkness at all. He has been here all along and is **perfect.** Oh boy! That's enough credentials for me!

Here's the deal: I am not worried about God's durability, I'm concerned about mine. I am not always trustworthy (forgot to pick up Winnie from ballet last night!). I don't have all the right answers (although I like to think I do). It's not easy for me to climb on the back seat when I like to know where I am going. I like being in charge and in control. I will even confess that sometimes I doubt God's direction. When it comes to **A-lignment**, I need to be first in line.

In 6th grade, I broke my right arm chasing boys up a tree. I know. I know. Hindsight is foresight. My eyes were looking up at the boys and not on the limb that was too unstable to hold me. I came crashing down. All nine feet. I braced the fall with my right arm and crack . . . no more alignment. I remember to this day the pain of the novocaine shot injected into my wrist to place it back into alignment. _Ouch._

The same is true when we are out of alignment with our Captain. **Our life hurts.** Sometimes it's easy to see, but often it's more subtle than a bone out of place. We might have a sense something is out of balance, but it's hard to detect. We need **new eyes** to see from His perspective. Open our eyes, Lord, that we may see the wonderful things.

What are the obvious and subtle things in your life that keep you out of A-lignment and compete with God for your attention? Take some time and ask God to show you areas in your life that you might need to change.

_____

_____

_____

_____

What is competing for your attention according to the following verses? What should your response be to allow God to steady your life?

Our Competition/ Our Response

- **John 12:43-46**

_____/_____
_____/_____

- **Ephesians 4:29**

_____/_____
_____/_____

- **Ephesians 4:31-5:2**

_____/_____
_____/_____
_____/_____

I like to call anything that distracts our attention from God, Kingdom competitors. These competitors desire mans' approval over God's approval. (This is biblical slang for people pleasing.) Unwholesome talk always tears people down and reveals our judgmental hearts. Gossip never builds up our friendships. Anger, bitterness, and rage destroy our A-lignment with God. Trusting in the things of this world for our balance will leave us miserable and empty. If we desire to be in continual communication with God, He **promises** to steady the bike for us. It's our choice. Every time we choose to hold our tongue, we choose to hop on the back and let God steer our circumstance. Every time we refrain from anger and rage, we choose to give God the control of our emotional state. Kingdom competitors are **false power sources.** They distract us from following God's lead and leave us at the bottom of a tree with a broken branch and a broken arm. We are out of A-lignment and our souls hurt.

Ephesians 5:1-2 gives us a solution for tandem toppling. It's living a life of love, imitating Christ, and being a fragrant aroma. Girls, we aren't smellin' so good when we seek praise from men, gossip, and stress about how overwhelmed and overcommitted we are. THIS IS FALSE POWER and leads to insecure and out of alignment living. 1 John 1:5 says that God is light. He is the true light source with lasting staying power. He is steadying the bike for us each day. He is our DURACELL®. We need to be A-ligned with Him and Him only to avoid **tandem toppling.**

Lord, thank You that You are waiting to steady me each and every day. You are the only power source I need. Help me when I get unbalanced and want to be in the control seat. Please convict me when I am swayed to gossip, anger, people pleasing, and discontent. You are so faithful. You are the truth. Teach me to believe and trust that Your leading is perfect. You see the road ahead and will lead me in the right direction. I love You, Jesus. You are unchanging. You are the perfect Captain. Help me not to tandem topple! Amen.

I RIDE
for PRAYER
REQUESTS

1. Look up and write down Romans 3:22-24.

It's so easy to get out of A-lignment with God. What does this verse tell you about being made right with God?

Our belief in Jesus Christ A-ligns us with God. We are made **right** with Him when we confess with our lips that He is Lord and trust that His life, death, and resurrection has the power to take away our sin. We have **all** fallen short of His glory. Therefore, no other power source will do. Jesus is the **only** power source we need. Our personal response to **who Jesus is** changes the direction of our course and destines us for eternity. When we choose Jesus, we are choosing to be made right with God, to A-lign ourselves to His leading, and to agree to our position on the back seat. But this is not the end!

The choice to believe in Christ is where the journey **begins!** Yes, we are saved from sin and have the guarantee of eternal life, but this is not all there is. We are saved to live out an abundant life for Christ—right here on earth.

35

2. Look up and write down Philippians 2:12b-13.

* What does this say about living an abundant life for Christ? Who is working in you?

Yes! **God** Himself, the Almighty Captain, IS working IN us. Notice the present tense. God **is** currently active in our lives through the person of the Holy Spirit. After Jesus ascended into heaven, the Holy Spirit came in full force to take His place—not in bodily form, but in spirit. He came to empower us, guide us, teach us, lead us, and plant in us God's desire to share the gospel and do His will. When we understand that the full power of Jesus is living **in us,** we will understand that life is to be lived to the fullest in this present moment! This is where **Riding Tandem** gets exciting! When we believe in Christ, HE LIVES IN US. But, we must be warned, as tandem riders, we need to be on the look out for Kingdom competitors.

* WARNING! Read John 10:9-10. Who wants to steal this abundant life?

Satan is a deceiver and wants us to believe that even though we have accepted Christ, we don't really need Him every day. We find ourselves saving our Christianity for just Sundays, Sunday School, saying our prayers at night, and going to Bible study (if we don't have a lot of homework). For the most part, we think we are just fine pedaling on our own. After all, we enjoy being on the front seat until we feel that something is missing. When Jesus becomes just a religion, a tradition, and our faith seems artificial, we begin to feel empty inside, defeated, and useless. Do you ever feel this way? Sister, I am here to tell you **there is hope!** Jesus saved you to live an ABUNDANT life. He saved you so you could have freedom and protection in His pasture. He saved you so you could ride—hands free—tandem with Him.

3. What do you think it takes to stay in alignment?

(Look at your life specifically to answer this question.)

* Look up Colossians 4:2. What are the three action steps we need to take to stay in alignment with God?

1.

2.

3.

+ PRAYER:

* What do you think it means to be devoted in prayer?

Praying with devotion is being **committed** to something. Praying with devotion is being unwilling to move, to be **steadfast.** Praying with devotion is **to press in** on . . . even when it's hard. Praying with devotion is **aligning** yourself with a godly perspective. The root word for devotion is to have **strength.** The idea of being devoted in prayer describes someone with **durable power.**

* Who in your life has a durable prayer life? What stands out to you in this person's character?

+ Watchful

* What do you think it means to be watchful when you pray?

Watchful means: to give strict attention to, to be cautious, to be awake.[3] The word watchful is used many times in the Old Testament describing men who were watching out for the enemy. Watch guards were usually stationed on high walls where they could get a better perspective. This allowed them to be the first to see the enemy approaching. These men were awake and always on the lookout for Kingdom competitors. They gave strict attention to their calling. When we combine these two actions together, devoting ourselves to prayer and being watchful at the same time, we will see from a new perspective, a godly perspective. We will see from a different level, a higher level, so we can be on the **lookout for the enemy** who tries to deceive us with false power. Devotion to prayer and being watchful **A-ligns us with God's perspective** so we can see the things God is doing in our life.

* How are you going to be on the lookout and see from a new perspective, God's perspective, as you watch and pray?

+ Thankful

* Why do you think it's important to be thankful when you pray?

Thankfulness is the foundation for staying in A-lignment with God. Why? Because life is hard and circumstances can be heartbreaking. Sometimes it takes God's "Duracell® power" to be thankful and "see" from His perspective—especially when our prayers don't turn out the way we expect. One thing is for sure, we can't do it by ourselves. We need our Captain's strength and perspective to keep us from tandem toppling. He's got the power and authority. When we trust that God is steering our circumstances and lean on Him with thanksgiving when life is not easy, **we stay in A-lignment.** Prayer. Watchful eyes. Thankful hearts.

4. What do you need to be thankful for today?

* (Note: Even in difficulty we need to be thankful. If you are going through a difficult time, list 3 things you can be thankful for?

Week FOUR: ALIGNMENT (Part 2)

ICE BREAKER Questions

1. Which letter of the alphabet describes you best? (Interesting, isn't it?)

2. What is the worst haircut you have ever had?

JOURNAL review

STOP and take five to ten minutes to discuss your journal time. How did these Scriptures help you to ride tandem with God this week?

IT's TIME TO RIDE: Group Lesson

Today we are going to see a biblical character who graduates from Christian Kindergarten and ends up with her Masters in Divinity—Queen Esther.

To give you a brief update, Esther is the Queen of Persia and the wife to King Xerxes. Mordecai is a Jew and also Esther's cousin who raised her after her parents died. The story unfolds as Mordecai finds out that an evil man named Haman has set a decree to "destroy, kill, and annihilate all the Jews— young and old, women and little children—on a single day, the thirteenth day of the twelfth month . . ." (Esther 3:13). Mordecai is found at the city gates in sack cloth, wailing and crying when Esther learns about the situation.

Please read Esther 4:1-17. (It's long but worth it!)

What is Esther's first response when she learns about Mordecai's distress? (Esther 4:4-5)

_____

_____

_____

What is Esther's first reaction when she learns of the decree and what Mordecai wants her to do? (Esther 4:10-11)

_____

_____

_____

What is Mordecai's response to her initial complaint? (Esther 4:12-14)

_____

_____

_____

How did Esther graduate from the Kindergarten of faith and move with power and perseverance to get her Master's degree? (Esther 4:15-5:1)

_____

_____

_____

When Queen Esther learns of the decree to annihilate the Jews, (an edict which could not be reversed because of the king's signature approval), we see her frightened and afraid. Her response to Mordecai was something like this: "You want me to do what? Dude, you **do** know I will be killed instantly if I walk in front of the King unannounced? He hasn't called for me in three weeks and . . . Mordecai, are you crazy?" I doubt the conversation went like that, but you get the picture!

Mordecai sends her this response—one that dog ears the pages of many Bibles including mine.

> "Do not think that because you are in the king's house you alone of all the Jews will escape. For if you remain silent at this time, relief and deliverance for the Jews will arise from another place, but you and your father's family will perish. And who knows but that you have come to royal position for such a time as this?"
>
> ESTHER 4:13-14

Esther was at a crossroads with a serious decision to make. If we reflect back to the journal question on page 15, Esther had the same decision the disciples had when Jesus asked them, "Who do **you** say that I am?" Who was God to Esther? Was He just a myth? Was He just a childhood fairy tale that Mordecai had taught her day in and day out? Were the stories of Abraham, Isaac, and Jacob really true? Could God be trusted in a time like this? Was she going to take control and steer this journey? Or was she going to trust God, believe in the miracles of the past, and get on the back of the tandem and pedal?

This is a great question for all of us.

What does our faith look like when we cannot see the road ahead, decisions need to be made, action needs to be taken, life is hectic, and the journey is scary? Do we choose to put our own agendas and selfish ambitions first? Or do we walk in wisdom, trusting that God is faithful?

_____
_____
_____
_____
_____
_____

• Do we have BAND-AID faith—a quick solution that covers up the pain so we can pretend it's not there? Or is our faith BOLD—willing to surrender our agendas, our comfort, and trust God with the impossible?

• Do we have APATHETIC faith—hoping with time the problem will just disappear? Or is our faith AUTHENTIC—recognizing the problem, our weakness, and CALL on God to empower us so we can align ourselves with His perspective?

Read Esther 4:15-17 and discuss/write down where you can see her A-lignment happening. Keep in mind: Devotion to prayer, being watchful, and thankful.

_____
_____
_____
_____
_____
_____

I love that Esther does not let the "Kingdom competitors" influence her actions. She does not ask Mordecai for advice. She doesn't ask her friends for advice. She doesn't text her latest drama or post

on social media. She decides to A-lign herself with the movement of her circumstance, praying, watching, and trusting that her Captain will lead her in the right direction. She is pedaling for her life. We see Esther go through a complete character change from a scared little queen to an **empowered daughter of the King.** We see her graduate from:

- Devastated to DEVOTED
- Problematic to PRAYERFUL
- Worried to WATCHFUL
- Terrified to THANKFUL

Esther gathers her maids together and asks Mordecai to gather ALL the Jews who are in Susa to PRAY and FAST for her—to not eat or drink for three days or nights. She makes the BOLD decision that when the time of fasting is over, she will approach the king unannounced even if it's against the law and her life is on the line.

When you cannot see the road ahead, do you post on social media or call on your friends to pray for you? What is going on in your life right now that prompts you to take off the band-aid and move to bolder faith? What have you learned in Riding Tandem that can empower your faith from apathetic to authentic?

_____
_____
_____
_____
_____
_____
_____
_____
_____
_____
_____
_____
_____
_____

Lord, thank You for the example of Queen Esther. I am also thankful that someone else gets scared to step into the unknown. Thank You for teaching me that through being watchful, prayerful, and thankful, I can change my faith from apathetic to authentic. Keep me in line with Your teachings so I can step out in faith with Your power in me. Today I choose to lean into Your leading and Ride Tandem with You. Amen.

I RIDE
for PRAYER
REQUESTS

1. Look up and write down the following verses.

* Write down how God reveals Himself to us on a personal level. What are His actions? What are our responses?

GOD's Action/OUR Response

• Isaiah 41:10

• Exodus 14:13-14

* How has God revealed Himself to you lately?

Our relationship with God is a **personal** one. Our tandem journey is built for two. Esther grew up in the Jewish faith just as many of us have grown up in a "Christian" home, but there comes a point in **all** of our lives when we have to decide who Jesus is . . . to us. Not our friends. Not our parents. But, to us—personally. This was Esther's moment. God was holding out His hand and steadying the bike for the Queen. He does the same for us.

2. Let's look at Psalm 119:18 again.
What does the word "open" mean to you?

> "Open my eyes
> that I may SEE
> the WONDERFUL
> things in
> your law"
>
> PSALM 119:18

Can you believe the word for open means: to reveal, to uncover, to make known? As she sat in the presence of the Lord opening her eyes **to see,** He was uncovering His plan for her. Esther was filling up with amazing power to go before the King . . . in the power of THE KING.

God reveals His plans when we are still enough to **pray, watch, and have thankful hearts** to obediently step into His plan. Three days of fasting with God empowered Esther to step with boldness into a powerless situation. Why do I say this? Esther had no authority—even as the Queen going before her husband unannounced. This proves a good point. In God's economy, we don't need the world's positioning. We only need God's **power.**

Imagine if Esther was impulsive and went before the king to declare her cause **before** three days of prayer and fasting. Hmmm. I think we might have a different ending! When we have decisions to make, it is critical to sit before the King of Kings and ask Him to reveal His plan for us to pursue. Don't be impulsive and pedal in your own strength. Take note of Esther's position of prayer, open your eyes, fast, ask your friends for prayer, and sit in the stillness of the Lord. Here's a truth to ride on:

If God is revealing something to you, He wants to DO something through you.

* Have you ever made an impulsive decision? How would it have been different if you had prayed first, like Esther?

3. Do you have BIG challenges ahead of you?

* How will you take the time to be prayerful, watchful, and thankful in this challenge? Consider a time of fasting and praying.

A fast can be anything—no soda, or sugar, or social media, or fast food. Something meaningful that when you miss it you will be reminded to stop, pray, and communicate with God. God is waiting to give you the same power He gave Esther.

4. What if you had a journal like Esthers?

It's always a good exercise to REMEMBER the faithfulness of the Lord especially when making a big decision. It is also a great idea to keep a journal for this very reason. Personal journals help us look back and SEE where God has led us—even when we were scared, unsure, angry, discouraged, or confused. We can read and **remember** where God held our hand, steadied our bike, and did not let us tandem topple. I am not saying the outcome will always be what we desire. But, if we are believers in Jesus, we can rest in the promise of knowing that God's plans for us are **good** (Jeremiah 29:11).

* Consider these four questions when making a big decision:

- FIRST COLUMN: What is the situation, and what is the decision you need to make?
- SECOND COLUMN: If you were in control, what actions would you take?
- THIRD COLUMN: Because God is in control, how are you going to obey His leading?
- FOURTH COLUMN: Write down God's faithfulness in this situation.

I'll get us started, but eventually grab a blank journal (hint: Journal Art Project on page 145!) and make your own columns. This is a great exercise! When we are in tune to God through devotion in prayer, being watchful, and giving thanks, we are in **A-lignment** and **Riding Tandem** with Him.

Situation	Actions	Obedience	Faithfulness

Esther's Beauty treatment

Milk and Honey Face Mask Recipe

Yogurt

Honey

Oatmeal

Bowl

Milk

INGREDIENTS

* 2 tbsp oatmeal (finely ground)
* 1 tbsp Greek Yogurt
* 1 tsp honey
* 2 tsp milk

Mix all ingredients together in a large bowl. Apply to clean face and leave on 5 minutes. Scrub the face in small circles, then rinse the face with warm water and pat the skin dry.

Fun fact: As a natural moisturizer, honey plays a role in natural cosmetics today as well as in Esther's time.

I PEDAL for SPA TREATMENTS

ICE BREAKER Questions

I break for ICE BREAKERS

1. What would you do in your life if you knew you could not fail?

2. If you sat down next to Jesus on a bus, what would you talk about?

JOURNAL review

STOP and take five to ten minutes to discuss your journal time. How did these Scriptures help you to ride tandem with God this week?

IT's TIME TO RIDE: Group Lesson

Week three is about N-ecessary Stops. While A-lignment is essential to balance us on our ride with Jesus, taking N-ecessary Stops gives us time to regroup, slow down, and reassess the direction we are headed.

However, some of us don't like to stop (ahem, me), or we don't feel we have the time to stop. Our lives are so hurry-hurry we just don't have the space in our day to add one more thing. The only problem with this riding strategy is that we will miss Jesus' work in our lives. We will become exhausted, over-stressed, and burned out. Remember, our Captain knows more about us than we do, and He knows when enough is enough. Here's my advice. When the Captain stops the bike, you better stop, too. Otherwise you are going to fly over the handlebars or find yourself pedaling ninety to nothin'—for nothin'. To have complete trust in our Captain, we have to have **complete trust** in His N-ecessary Stops.

Today, we are going to be studying Luke 24:13-35. To set the stage, Jesus has been arrested, crucified, and resurrected. Word is leaking out that some women, who were going to prepare the body with spices, found the tomb empty. We pick up the story and find two men walking to a village called Emmaus. While talking about everything that had just happened, Jesus comes up and walks **with them**, yet, they do not recognize Him.

Read Luke 24:13-35.

What do you think the men were discussing when Jesus walked beside them?

_____

_____

What was the overall demeanor of the men? (Luke 24:17)

_____

_____

Why do you think Jesus wanted a re-cap of all that was happening?

_____

_____

What was the hope of these two men? (Luke 24:21)

_____

_____

What was the final response of Jesus? (Luke 24:25-26)

_____

_____

What was the clue that opened their eyes to reveal it was actually Jesus who was with them all the time? (Luke 24:30-32)

_____

_____

N-ecessary Stops give us eyes to see with a **new perspective**. When we are walking too fast or preoccupied with our own agendas, we can't see that our Captain is right in front of us! Just ask these two men walking to Emmaus. I love what Jesus says to them in verse 25. The word for foolish comes from the Greek word "morosh," and it's where we get the word moron. Not what you expect your Captain to lean back and call you, right? But I bet it would get your attention! It got mine.

Here's what struck me. These men **knew** the words of the prophets. Good grief! They probably memorized the words of the Torah as boys. But because they were walking in their own opinions of what happened, they were distracted from the truth. These men thought Jesus was going to save them from the oppression of Rome and come forth as a King to rescue them. **They had it all wrong.** Jesus did come to save and He was a King, but He did not come to rescue Israel from political tyranny.

He came to save us from the destitution of our sins. The freedom Jesus was offering was more than a freedom from Rome. It was a freedom from the chains of sin and separation from God. His death on the cross paid the penalty of our brokenness that began ALL the way back with the disobedience of Adam and Eve.

Here's what else struck me. **TIME.** Can you imagine the time it took for Jesus to start at the beginning and tell the **whole** story from Moses and all the Prophets concerning Himself? I would guess about seven miles. What a great question to ponder while considering the N-ecessary Stops in Riding Tandem. We need to **stop** and **walk** with Jesus. He's got all the time in the world! Here's the best part. Jesus cares enough to stop us not only when our faith gets "cattywhompus," but also to teach us, counsel us, and steer us in the right direction.

Why do you think Jesus appeared to these two men to walk alongside and spend the next seven miles explaining His story?

_____

_____

_____

N-ecessary Stops **open our eyes** to see Jesus. When we don't understand why things are happening, I think we like to put our own spin to it. When we are disappointed the way life is turning out, we like to try to take control or believe in the opinions of others. This is dangerous territory. Be careful. To understand the truth of Scripture and have wisdom in the situations we don't understand, we need to stop and take lots of walks with Jesus. When we speed through life, four things can happen:

> "When he was at the table with them, he took bread, gave thanks, broke it and began to give it to them. Then their eyes were opened and they recognized him, ...They asked each other, "Were not our hearts burning within us while he talked with us on the road and opened the Scriptures to us?"
>
> LUKE 24:30-32

- We miss seeing Jesus right in front of us.
- We forget God's promises.
- The truth is distorted.
- We believe what we want to believe (even if it opposes Scripture)

- This is a bonus: We will be morons.

I do not want to be a moron. But this requires me to take N-ecessary Stops and spend time with Jesus. While we can't walk with Jesus physically anymore, we can read His Word and be inspired by the Holy Spirit. The same Jesus that showed up at dinner is living inside of us (Romans 8:10-11). We, too, can sense the same overwhelming power. "Were not our hearts burning within us while he talked with us on the road and opened the Scriptures to us?"

Jesus is so cool. I want to go on a seven mile walk with Him. I love that He has the time for me to do this. The question is, do I?

Last February, our family went to Disney World. As I approached the front of this very long line, a Disney man took me aside and said, "Are you a Florida resident? Wait here." As I was waiting, six other people went ahead of me! I was just about to express my opinion about being hoodwinked when the nice Disney man took me to a back window and said with a smile, "It's quicker to wait."

What on earth? As I left the line with my Animal Kingdom pass, I couldn't get his comment out of my head. It's quicker to wait? I don't think so Mr. Disney worker. But as I chewed on his comment for a while, I began to think that Smiley had a good point.

Read this passage from one of my favorite devotionals *Streams in the Desert* from May 17th:

> "The hours spent waiting are not lost time. Quite often God will ask us to wait before we go, so we may fully recover from our last mission before entering the next stage of our journey and work." [5]

I call this a N-ecessary Stop. Far too often we want to jump into the next activity, the next sport, or the next opportunity. But sometimes, God wants us to pause and take a break. Maybe He wants us to stop and wait. Because if it's not God's timing, you will waste your time. **It's quicker to wait.**

Today, He is waiting for you. He yearns to teach you and explain His story. He wants to show you all His promises so when you SEE them, your heart will burn within you. Don't be distracted by the world's opinions. Seek His wisdom and it will be graciously given to you (James 1:3). Take the clues of N-ecessary Stops and stop pedaling. He has so much to teach us, but first we need to slow down, get off the bike, and listen. He's right beside you.

What do you think it means to be quicker to wait? Have you ever "missed" Jesus in front of you? How are you going to take a N-ecessary Stop?

_____

_____

_____

Dear Lord, thank You for teaching me about N-ecessary Stops this week. Why is it so hard to stop, Lord? I think it's because deep down I like the activity and often feel more accepted when I am busy. Thank You for opening my eyes to see that I need stops to walk with You. I need stops to talk with You. I need stops to change my perspective. I need stops to distinguish between public opinion and truth. Allow me to recognize YOU this week and to remember Your promises. Thank You for the freedom to not always understand, but to know that You are always walking beside me. Open my heart and my eyes to recognize You, today. Amen.

I RIDE
for PRAYER
REQUESTS

1. Have you ever stepped ahead of God and taken matters into your own hands? What happened?

I remember the day in kindergarten when Gareth Bond dared me to bite him. "What?" I said. "You're kidding, right?" "Nope," Gareth teased. **"I don't think you will do it."** SO—with a super strong will and a harder bite, I took a chunk out of his arm. He screamed to high heaven, told the teacher, and I was sent to the Principal's office for the first time in my life. My reason? He told me to do it! Taking matters into your own hands without taking a N-ecessary Stop is never a good idea.

Sometimes we decide that God is not doing things our way, or meeting our deadlines, or expectations. So what do we do? We step out and make things happen. In our own way. In our own timing. In our complete control. But the result is a complete **bike wreck**.

We can plan, plan, plan, or bite, bite, bite all we want, but it is the Lord who determines our steps and STOPS.

> N-ecessary Stops **to believe** in the promises of God. (Psalm 90:12)
>
> N-ecessary Stops **to know** that God has ordained each day for us. (Psalm 39:4)
>
> N-ecessary Stops **to ask** for wisdom because life is short. (Psalm 139:13-14)

*{Dig Deeper} Read the following verses above and write down why N-ecessary Stops are so important.

• Psalm 90:12

- Psalm 39:4

- Psalm 139:15-16

2. N-ecessary Stops are essential to our ride on the tandem bike. Here's another reason why.

When we slow down to stop, we can look into our past and **see** where God has been faithful. This is especially important when the road ahead seems dim. To press ahead, God wants us to remember His faithfulness. N-ecessary Stops help us to slow down and be encouraged to see that He was there all along. Unfortunately, our tendency can be to take quick glances into our rear view mirror when life is full steam ahead. The problem is this: Steam sets on the mirror and God's blessings get foggy in our lives.

* Has remembering God's faithfulness ever been foggy? Looking back in your past, how has God been faithful? — especially during a difficult time?

Remember: God is always with you in this tandem ride through life.

This bicycle is built for two.

3. Read Exodus 15:11-13 and Exodus 16:1-16.

* How do the Israelite's praise the Lord in Exodus 15:11?

> "Then the Lord said to Moses, 'I will rain down bread from heaven for you. Everyday the people must go out and gather what they NEED for the day.'"
>
> EXODUS 16:4 (NLT)

* How had the Israelite's attitude changed in Exodus 16:3? What do they think of God in this verse? Why?

* How did God continue to provide for them after some serious hissy fits?

Whining. Grumbling. Complaining. The Israelites were experts at complaining. Just one chapter before the grumbling, they were talking about the majesty and wonder of the Lord **until** their comforts were challenged. The word **until** spoke loud and clear to me.

> They were delighting in the Lord . . . **until** their stomach's gurgled.
> They were praising God for all His glory . . . **until** they were uncomfortable.

Do you honestly think the Israelites wanted to go back into slavery and suppression under Pharaoh? No way. These until moments are good N-ecessary Stops for all of us to consider. Why? They test the foundation of our faith.

Until moments happen when one minute you are praising the Lord for all of His glory. Life is great. God is great. And, the next minute you are not so sure He even cares.

God was my rock and foundation, UNTIL my best friend didn't include me at her birthday party.

God was always there for me, UNTIL my parents got divorced.

God was my song, UNTIL I broke my leg in soccer.

4. Have you ever had an until moment? How can a N-ecessary Stop help you build your faith?

Whatever your UNTIL moment, today is a good reason to stop. **God is with you.** N-ecessary Stops help us to evaluate and remember that God is indeed good.

* Read Hebrews 11:1. How is faith defined?

When we cannot SEE God at work, faith sees for us. We have hope and conviction that our Captain is taking us to the place He desires us to be. It's not always the destination God is concerned about, but rather the **journey to get us there.** This is where real life lessons are learned.

5. How can the following verses remind us that God is faithful in the UNTIL moments?

- **Psalm 86:15**

"But you, O Lord, are a God merciful and gracious, slow to anger and abounding in steadfast love and faithfulness." Psalm 86:15

- **Deuteronomy 7:9**

- **1 Corinthians 1:9**

"God is faithful, by whom you were called into the fellowship of his Son, Jesus Christ our Lord." 1 Corinthians 1:9

- **1 Corinthians 10:13**

Dear Lord, thank You that You are indeed faithful. Even when I cannot see the road clearly, I know You are my Captain and are steering my tandem bike. You are steadfast when I am shaky. You are full of mercy when I am meandering. You are leading when I am lopsided. You are faithful. Give me the desire to slow down and take a good look into my past where I can see Your unswerving guidance. Remind me each morning, as I ride into my day, that You are leading me into Your ways. And, Lord, when I have those UNTIL moments, please steady the bike for me. You are my Captain. Let's enjoy this stop together. Amen.

Week SIX: N-ECESSARY STOPS (part 2)

ICE BREAKER Questions

I break for ICE BREAKERS

1. If you could change anything about yourself, what would you change and why?

2. Have you ever been "hangry?" -- when you are so hungry that you get angry. What happened?

JOURNAL review

STOP and take five to ten minutes to discuss your journal time. How did these Scriptures help you to ride tandem with God this week?

IT's TIME TO RIDE: Group Lesson

Today, we are going to back pedal a little. There are just too many lessons the Israelites experienced in their UNTIL moments not to go back and learn from them.

There are three things we will learn today from the N-ecessary Stop God made the Israelites take. I think we will all be able to identify.

1. Hunger exaggerates complaining.
2. God continues to provide for us even when we complain.
3. Knowing and Seeing.

Open your Bible are read Exodus 16:3 again. In your opinion, why would this statement be a bit exaggerated?

_____

_____

_____

_____

_____

Empty stomachs magnify our emotions—at least they do in our family! Empty stomachs make us "hangry"(a combination of hungry and angry). On a side note, I am convinced that all children (including the Israelites) have the universal middle name "starving." Mine do!

> "Hi John John. How was your day?" **I'm starving.**
> "Great to see you Curry, Jr.! How was football?" **I'm starving.**
> "Winnie, how was ballet?" **I'm starving.**
> "Daley! How was the Bible Study with the girls?" **I'm starving.**

And, of course, if your house is like ours, there is never ANYTHING to eat. Don't get me wrong. I am not trying to be hard on my kids. When I am hungry, my emotions tend to reach a high level too. How about you?

POINT TWO: God continues to provide for us even when we complain.

Reread Exodus 16:4 and visualize the overwhelming compassion of the Lord.

Amazing! God hears our complaining and STILL provides all that we need. The NIV translation says, "they will gather enough for that day." Notice this verse does not say everything they **wanted.** Big difference. Goodness. If God gave the Israelites what they wanted, they would be back eating all they desired in Egypt (vs. 3). NOT. Maybe hunger makes us hallucinate too—making our past look dreamy and magical. Warning: This is a ploy of the enemy. His purpose from the beginning of time has been to try to get us to believe that God is not good enough. Don't be lured into his web of lies. **God is enough. He is good enough. He will ALWAYS be enough.** He will continue to rain down His compassion on us. Every day. All day. Take that Satan.

N-ecessary Stops help us to identify the lies.

Read the following verses. Why does God provide what we need and not necessarily what we want?

- **Psalm 23:1-3**

_____

_____

_____

- **Philippians 4:19**

_____

_____

_____

- **2 Corinthians 9:8**

_____

_____

_____

The Lord is our Shepherd and our Captain. He knows what we need and will not leave us on the side of the road. He protects us and will generously provide **enough** for us. In fact, He will supply so much that we will have leftovers! I needed to hear this today. I also needed to hear that God's love is not conditional. My behavior never tips the scale of His unconditional love for me. He never thinks, "Well, it looks like Annie is trying to steer her circumstances again, I think I'll just opt-out for sending her compassion today." No way. This is not God's nature. God's love never changes. It is unconditional. Read Psalm 145:9.

> "The LORD is good to everyone. He showers compassion on all his creation." PSALM 145:9

YES. Even in our sinful, complaining, over-exaggerating, selfish-selves, GOD is still good. He is still showering His compassion on ALL His creation. One of my favorite art projects I have created comes from one of my tween Bible studies called The Perfect Present. In the first lesson, we study God's character with the acronym of G.I.F.T.— God is **G**-reat. God is **I**-nfinite. God is our **F**-ather. And God is **T**-ruth. The art project for the day? Umbrellas! Why? Because God showers His compassion on all His creation!

POINT THREE: Knowing and Seeing.

This third point might seem a bit obscure to learn from Israel's N-ecessary Stop, but when we reread Exodus 16:6-7, you will see the direction we are headed.

> "So Moses and Aaron said to all the men, 'This evening you will KNOW that the Lord is the one who brought you out of Egypt. Tomorrow morning you will SEE the greatness of the Lord." EXODUS 16:6-7

Even in the wilderness of the Israelite's complaining and over-exaggeration, the Lord rained down compassion by giving them manna in the morning and quail in the evening. Can you imagine the miracle? In this N-ecessary Stop, they experienced the greatness of the Lord. They **knew** the greatness. They **saw** the greatness. **Knowing and seeing—** exactly in that order. This is imperative to our lesson— and our **N-ecessary Stop.**

We must first KNOW God in order to SEE His miracles.

My question is this: What will it take for you to KNOW God first, in order to SEE Him working in your life?

_____

_____

_____

_____

I am not talking about knowing about Him, but knowing Him personally and experientially. We need to know that God is enough and that He abundantly provides for our every need. We need to know enough about Him . . .

- **To stop** our complaining.
- **To trust** Him in the "I'm hungry" times.
- **To believe** in His goodness in the "I don't understand" times.
- **To have the faith** to know that God is steering our tandem bike when we hit those "UNTIL" moments.
- **To identify** the truth from the lies.

What will it take for us to KNOW God? Will it take a miracle? Walking on water? Watching an ocean part so we can cross on dry land? Will it take watching food appear in the morning and evening to satisfy our hunger? Even in these amazing mountaintop moments when God displayed His power, the Israelites lost faith. We will, too. All they wanted in their UNTIL moment was to return to the valley of exaggerated complaining, believing they were better off not having been rescued at all. Do we lose faith this quickly, too?

How do you react when God allows a difficult season in your life?

_____

_____

_____

I am always moved when I hear Lauren Daigles's song, *Trust in You*.[6] Take a N-ecessary Stop and download this song on to your playlist. For now, enjoy these few lines:

```
           Truth is you know what tomorrow brings
         There's not a day ahead you have not seen
           So let all things be my life and breath
         I want what you want Lord and nothing less

             When you don't move the mountains
                   I'm needing you to move
              When you don't part the waters
                 I wish I could walk through
             When you don't give the answers
                    As I cry out to you
     I will trust, I will trust, I will trust in you
                   I will trust in you
```

Until we **KNOW** our Captain and believe in His strength, power, love, compassion, and desire for us to get us where He wants us to go, we will not **SEE** nor understand why or where He is leading us. Jesus said, "I am the bread of life. Whoever comes to me will never go hungry, and whoever believes in me will never be thirsty" (John 6:35). We might not have manna in the morning and quail in the evening, but **we do have the Word of God to sustain us.** We never have to be hangry again. God commands us not to complain or argue (Philippians 2:14). This is why we need N-ecessary Stops. We have to FILL up with God's promises so that when we hit those hangry, complaining, until, "mountains-don't-move" moments, we have God's Word to speak into our empty places.

As we close, consider this. **Are you hungry for something the Lord has not given to you? Has a mountain not moved in your life? Is your appetite for more consuming your thoughts? Or are you satisfied with provision He has given you?**

_____
_____
_____
_____
_____

Dear Lord, thank You for Your overflowing compassion for Your children. Even in our rotten attitudes, You continue to love us. I pray that today's N-ecessary Stop will open our eyes to the truth of Your Word and will destroy the lies that invade our minds. The truth of Your Word is the best weapon we have to fight our "hangry" dispositions, bitter hearts, and complaining attitudes. Our desire is to KNOW You and to SEE the evidence of Your hand in our lives. Help us to understand that You are enough. Show us Your provision in our lives, today. Open our eyes to see the wonderful! Amen.

I RIDE
for PRAYER
REQUESTS

N-ecessary Stops are never intended so that we can have an excuse to quit or give up. No. N-ecessary Stops are meant to refresh our spirit and rely on God's faithfulness.

Let's turn to the good ole' story of David and Goliath. We are going to learn how to fight sticky situations with **uncommon solutions** and battles with **uncommon weapons.** Get ready. These are not the conventional weapons of this world. They are God's weapons.

Read 1 Samuel 17:17-58 and find out how one brother, one king, and one giant tried to discourage David from fighting Goliath.

* What did David's brothers say to him? What names did they call him? (1 Samuel 17:28)

* What was King Saul's response to David? (1 Samuel 17:33)

* How did Goliath try to humiliate David? (1 Samuel 17:41-44)

* What did David say in response to ALL these discouraging remarks? (1 Samuel 17:26, 1 Samuel 17:34-37, 1 Samuel 17:45-47)

* Before we learn the uncommon weaponry, what would you have used to fight back in this situation? Anger? Irritability? Attitude?

With every discouraging comment, David fought back with the power of God's promises. David spoke God's Word to his brothers, King Saul, and Goliath. He proclaimed that God has an army (vs. 26,45), God is a LIVING God (vs. 26), and that God will deliver the faithful (vs. 37,46). **God's promises are the uncommon weapons.**

N-ecessary Stops give us new eyes to see God at work, and He gives us **uncommon weapons** to fight common battles. It may not be easy. It may take discipline and hard work. But it's worth it. Remember, Riding Tandem is about the journey.

Jesus used the same weaponry when He was tempted by the devil in Matthew 4.

2. Read Matthew 4:1-11, first. Now read Jesus' responses in the New Living Translation.

Matthew 4:4
"But Jesus told him, "No! The Scriptures say, 'People do not live by bread alone, but by every word that comes from the mouth of God.'"

Matthew 4:7
Jesus responded, "The Scriptures also say, 'You must not test the Lord your God.'"

Matthew 4:10
"Get out of here, Satan," Jesus told him. "For the Scriptures say, 'You must worship the Lord your God and serve only him.'"

* What is the repeating phrase Jesus uses when tempted by the devil?

* How can you use this example of Christ the next time you are caught in a tempting situation?

Satan is not the truth. He's the big fat ugly giant trying to tell you that you can't win any battle with temptation and life is hopeless. Satan will try to convince you that God is not enough. When we know the truth of Scripture, we can fight back with **God's Promises.**

3. What giants are you facing today? Anger? A broken friendship? Past mistakes? Pride? Materialism? Wanting to be popular?

* How are you going to take a N-ecessary Stop to stock up on some Scripture and fight back with God's promises?

4. Let's look up some uncommon weaponry that we can use in our battles against giants. What are the uncommon weapons used to fight our battles?

• **Colossians 3:13-14**

- **Psalm 103:10**

  "He does not treat us as our sins deserve or repay us according to our iniquities." Psalm 103:10

- **Joshua 1:9**

- **Psalm 13:5**

These promises are just a fragment of God's arsenal. Don't use the weapons of anger, force, or manipulation to fight your battles, instead search the Word of God and ask the Holy Spirit to guide you in choosing the right one.

When someone hurts you, fight back with forgiveness.

"Make allowance for each other's faults, and forgive anyone who offends you. Remember, the Lord forgave you, so you must forgive others." Colossians 3:13 NLT

When someone mistreats you, fight back with God's mercy.

"He does not treat us as our sins deserve or repay us according to our iniquities." Psalm 103:10

When you are facing a giant, fight back with courage.

"Have I not commanded you? Be strong and courageous. Do not be terrified; do not be discouraged, for the LORD your God will be with you wherever you go." Joshua 1:9

When a situation is not going the direction you intended, fight back with **love.**

"But I trust in your unfailing love; my heart rejoices in your salvation." Psalm 13:5

The good news is this: **Jesus has already won the battle.** We need to lean into His leading and trust in His protection and direction for our lives. Every. Single. Day. Take N-ecessary Stops to know the TRUTH of Scripture. When someone says something hurtful, fight back with the uncommon weapons of God's promises.

5. In closing, write a prayer telling God what you have learned about N-ecessary Stops.

* Read Exodus 14:14. Use this verse to write down the promises you will use as You trust Him to fight your battles for you.

> "The LORD will fight for you; you need only to be still."
> EXODUS 14:14

N-ecessary Stops are necessary. They stop us to reassess, reevaluate, and remember that God is good. They slow us down to see Jesus walking beside us. They quiet our hearts to wait for God's perfect timing. They remind us that God is always there for us in those until moments. They expose our hangry, complaining, unthankful souls to change our perspective. They allow us to fill up on the power of God's Word so we can distinguish the truth from the lies. **They give us uncommon weaponry.**

My prayer is that we will take N-ecessary Stops often. Be on the alert when Jesus is slowing down the bike so you can get off and take a breather. It is worth it. He can make up the time. When we are rested, we can hop on the back and ride with confidence that Jesus, our Captain, has already won the battle.

Make a NO-SEW Fleece Blanket

Perfect for a bike ride to the park!

* Supplies:

2 yards patterned fleece
2 yards plain color fleece
Sharp fabric scissors

* Instructions:

1. Spread your fleece out on the floor, making sure to lay the patterned fleece on top of the plain color fleece. Smooth out wrinkles and match up edges as best you can.

2. Cut a five-inch square out of each of the four corners of your fleece

3. Begin cutting a row of strips or "fringe" on all four sides of the blanket. Cut through both layers of fabric at the same time. Fringe pieces should be about 1 1/2 inches wide and 4-5 inches long.

4. Now, take a top and bottom piece of each strip and tie a double knot, repeating all the way across.

5. Repeat steps 3 and 4 on the remaining three sides of the blanket until all four sides are knotted. Voila! It's that easy. It is essential to have a blanket for a N-ecessary Stop (or a beautiful day at the park!).

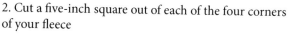

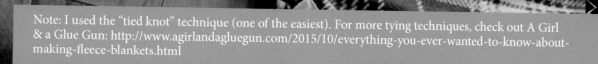

Note: I used the "tied knot" technique (one of the easiest). For more tying techniques, check out A Girl & a Glue Gun: http://www.agirlandagluegun.com/2015/10/everything-you-ever-wanted-to-know-about-making-fleece-blankets.html

Week SEVEN: D-on't Stop Pedaling

I break for ICE BREAKERS

1. If you could be in the movie of your choice, what movie would you choose and what character would you play?

2. If you could eliminate one thing from your daily schedule, what would it be and why?

JOURNAL review

STOP and take five to ten minutes to discuss your journal time. How did these Scriptures help you to ride tandem with God this week?

IT's TIME TO RIDE: Group Lesson

Today we are riding into D-on't Stop Pedaling. In review, we have prepared for T-ake off, A-ligned ourselves correctly, and realized the need for N-ecessary Stopping points.

I must interject that Riding Tandem was not the original name for this study. The first title was **LEAD.** Simple and to the point. I am not sure why I was drawn to this word, but it seemed that LEAD was in every verse I was studying. Has this ever happened to you? Take note. I believe God is trying to tell you something! Lead is used over and over again in the Old and New Testament. God will LEAD us. We will LEAD others. Others will LEAD us. We are called LEADers—both good and bad. It's a fascinating word search.

So what does LEAD have to do with our fourth chapter, D-on't Stop Pedaling? Read our first verse, Habakkuk 3:19 in the side margin and ride on.

The International Children's Bible reads, "He **leads** me safely on the steep mountains . . . ." The word for enable is *darak* meaning to cause or to LEAD.[7]

"The Sovereign Lord is my strength; he makes my feet like the feet of a deer, he enables me to tread on the heights. . ."

HABAKKUK 3:19 (NIV)

When you read the ICB translation of Habakkuk 3:19 in the margin, what two words pop out to you?

_____and _____

The two words that struck a cord for me were: STEEP and SAFELY. Makes you think, right? I am so glad God is leading!

Curry, Jr. was 7-years-old when he decided that his dad's directions down the mountain in Wyoming were not going to work for him. Why go up and away from the ranch when the direct path was down and to the right? Without asking permission, Curry, Jr. took off and blazed his own trail. By himself. My husband didn't budge, kept on walking, and let him go. I was not so calm. OK. I was freaking out. (In our family this is called a F.O. — a freak out!)

"Curry! You can't let a child go down a mountain by himself hoping he will make it back safely. It's steep, and who knows what is behind or **in** that sage bush?" I argued. We split up. Not by choice. Curry, Sr. took Winnie and John-John. I took Daley, and we started hiking down the mountain to find Curry. Needless to say, I was NOT a happy camper at this point. Not happy for my husband. Not happy for my son. What a joy I was to hike with!

We finally found little Curry. He was clearly frustrated that the path he had chosen was thorny and ankle deep in mud. More than that, admitting that his dad was right was really frustrating. We sure can get upset when we know someone else's choice was better all along! It's a pride thing, and it starts early.

Curry, Sr. knew the way. He was our leader. He also had hiked this mountain many times before. Yes, he knew the path looked steeper at first, but in the end, it was the safest way to the finish line. **Steep and safe.**

Winnie and John-John were skipping into the ranch singing "Mr. Bluebirds on my shoulder." When Daley, Curry, and I hit the finish line, I was singing, "You better get your rear end in the shower." It's not a good song. But, then again, I was not in a good mood either.

Here's my point. Curry Jr. hiked the path that **seemed** the quickest, easiest, and more direct. But he found out quickly that his decision was the wrong one. He should have followed his father.

According to Habakkuk 3:19, what does God give us when we follow His lead?

_____

_____

_____

How are we described?

_____

_____

_____

How does He LEAD us?

_____

_____

_____

I consider steep mountains to be those **difficult times in our lives** where we are at a crossroad. We can choose to go our own way, on a path that may seem more direct, easy, and quick. Or, we can choose to take a N-ecessary Stop and ask God for directions. The one credit I will give to little Curry was that he never gave up. He was pedaling for sure—but in his own power. That's never good. Pedaling on a tandem bike takes the work of two riders. Here is another amazing fact about the functionality of two people pedaling. **There is more power!** Have you ever tried to pedal alone on the back of a tandem while the front rider glides? It's near impossible, and not to mention **exhausting**.

God never intended for us to pedal alone. But, He did intend for us to pedal. We must press on and persevere through difficult times, not because we can pedal faster or harder, but because He is **helping** us pedal. Remember, He is our "Duracell"® power (chapter two, lesson one).

What do these verses say about allowing God to supply the power?

- **2 Chronicles 32:7**

"Be strong and courageous! Don't be afraid or discouraged because of the king of Assyria or his mighty army, for there is a power far greater on our side!" 2 Chronicles 32:7 (NLT)

_____

_____

- **Psalm 118:8**

_____

_____

- **Psalm 40:4**

_____

_____

_____

- **Matthew 19:26**

_____

_____

_____

- **Jeremiah 10:12**

_____

_____

_____

We will never make it through this ride of life if we depend on our own abilities. We can muster up all the power and might we have to get through a difficult situation, but in the end, we will have muddy feet and frustrated hearts. When we trust in the Lord's power, He will make our feet like a deer who skips along the rocky edges of the mountains. We will have courage and strength when the path looks too steep to climb. We will be blessed with endurance to press on knowing we are safe in His arms. If at first the path seems higher and out of sight, TRUST in the Captain. He has hiked this mountain before. All things are possible with God.

As we close today, think about a time when you did it your own way and pedaled in your own strength? What happened? Think also about a time when you trusted in God? What was the difference?

_____

_____

_____

_____

_____

_____

Dear Lord, thank You that You are my Captain who gives me the strength to pedal through difficult situations. You are my power source and my refuge in times of trouble. Nothing is impossible for You. Give me the wisdom to trust in You for all areas of my life, especially those where I am trying to pedal all by myself. It's hard, exhausting, and a losing battle. Lead me today, O Lord, safely through the difficulty of steep mountainous situations. Whether at work, at home, in relationships, unfulfilled desires, or broken dreams—with You as my Leader, I am sure to find strength, safety, and protection. Lead me, Lord, and equip me with Your Spirit. Amen.

I RIDE
for PRAYER
REQUESTS

1. Let's examine the word LEAD again.

* What do the following verses teach us about God's leading that guides us through the darkness of situations? (Choose one, or if you have time, look up all of them!)

• **Isaiah 42:16**

• **Isaiah 49:10**

• **Isaiah 58:8,11**

• **Exodus 15:13**
"In your unfailing love you will lead the people you have redeemed. In your strength you will guide them to your holy dwelling." Exodus 15:3

• **Isaiah 58:10-11**

• **Proverbs 3:5-7**
"Trust in the LORD with all your heart; do not depend on your own understanding. Seek his will in all you do, and he will show you which path to take. Don't be impressed with your own wisdom. Instead, fear the LORD and turn away from evil." Proverbs 3:5-7(NLT)

2. Which of these verses do you need to take to heart today?

Could it be the promise that God will lead you on unfamiliar paths and make the rough places smooth? Do you need to be reminded again that God has compassion for you? Do you need His strength and guidance? Do you need to trust Him more and depend less on your own ideas and agendas?

3. Use the space below to write a personal prayer telling God what you need today. Allow the power of these verses to lead you as you lean into Him.

4. Before we start today's lesson, let's review the positioning of the riders on the tandem as we continue to build our theme of D-on't Stop Pedaling.

"The captain is responsible for communicating with the stoker, calling out when to start pedaling, when to stop pedaling, when hazards or bumps are present in the road, when he is about to shift or brake, and any other information that the stoker needs to know. The stoker is responsible for listening to and following the captain's instructions without hesitation . . ." [8]

I love the last statement–**without hesitation.** Think about this for a minute.

How can you follow God's lead without hesitation?

Let's take a look at a very interesting component of the tandem called the **drive chain.** This is what Wikipedia says:

"To transfer power from all pedals to the rear wheel requires a drive train. Typically, the forward crankset is connected by a left-side timing chain to the rear crankset, which in turn is connected by a right-side chain to the rear wheel." [9]

This is Annie's interpretation—The drive train is required to transfer power to the REAR tire where we are positioned. Because it is connected to the **timing** chain, the drive chain has to have the right amount of **tension** to transfer the force to the rear wheel.

Tension and timing. Sounds Biblical to me!

God uses tension in our lives to deepen our dependence on Him. If there is no tension, we would never experience His power. However, I believe many Christians seem to feel disconnected to the power when we can't explain the tension, i.e., the pain, the trouble, or the misunderstanding. When we can't see the road ahead or we can't understand why God is taking us through a difficult time, doubt sets in and we lose our focus. Instead of having more faith, we begin to doubt the Captain's capabilities and our thoughts become fixated on the anxieties of our day. Worry gets in the front seat and faith is left behind.

5. Look up and read Psalm 22:1-3.

* At what point in these verses do you see the Psalmist shift from worry to trust? What do you think brought about this change?

*Look up and read Hebrews 4:14-16. Why do we hold firmly to our faith?

* How can we identify with Jesus?

* What is the basis upon which we can approach God's throne of grace with confidence?

* What is promised?

Love always keeps pedaling. Love was A-ligned and took a N-ecessary Stop on this earth to rescue man from eternal separation from a Holy God. **Love never gave up.** Regardless of incalculable affliction of the soul, Jesus laid down his life for you and for me.

In God's perfect timing, He sent His son to heal mankind's broken relationship that began in the garden through the disobedience of Adam and Eve. By believing in the perfect life, death, and resurrection of His Son, Jesus Christ, we can now enter God's throne room through prayer and have a personal relationship with Jesus. We can cry out to Him and be saved. We can trust in Him and not be put to shame. This was impossible in the Old Testament. Connection with Jehovah only happened once a year when the high priest would enter the Holy of Holies to confess the sins of the people. Today, we can approach the throne room because Jesus is our High Priest. We have 24 hour access.

We can pray. We can read His Word. We can fellowship with other believers—ALL because **Jesus is the DRIVE TRAIN.** He is the connection that allows us to Ride Tandem with the God of the universe!

The reason there is power available beyond our circumstances is because **Jesus is the power source.** When you are face to face with a mountain of difficulty, are you going to tell God how big your mountain is OR are you going to tell your mountain how BIG your God is? I love what Tony Evans says, "Faith is in your FEET, not in your feelings."[10] How true. We tend to get so wrapped up in our feelings, we forget to focus on the power source. We need to switch the focus from our feelings to faith. **Tension and timing.**

6. Look up and read Romans 8:28.

* What is the proof that tension and timing go hand in hand?

* When in your life has friction been a good thing? Did you see God's purpose in the tension and power in the timing?

What in your life was produced by a painful result of friction? Can you enter the throne room with confidence and cry aloud to your Captain? Can you allow the pressure of any situation to generate spiritual power? One thing is for certain. You can't do this riding alone. **You need Jesus.** When He is the drive train, the connection of power to the back rider, we can switch our . . . problems to **praise**, troubles to **trust**, worries to watching the **wonderful things**, and fear to **freedom.**

My friend Susan New said this, "Our obstacles are not an end to us finding God, but rather a pathway to allow Him to take us to higher places."

D-on't Stop Pedaling, my friend. There is perfect timing in the tension. Even if you feel, at times, disconnected to the power, Jesus is always steering you in the right direction. Lean into the power and trust in His leading. Amen!

"Be strong and courageous! Don't be afraid or discouraged because of the king of Assyria or his mighty army, for there is a power far greater on our side!"

2 CHRONICLES 32:7 (NLT)

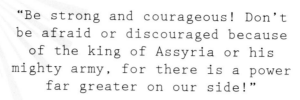

"Trust in the LORD with all your heart; do not depend on your own understanding. Seek his will in all you do, and he will show you which path to take. Don't be impressed with your own wisdom. Instead, fear the LORD and turn away from evil."

PROVERBS 3:5-7 (NLT)

"Love never gives up, never loses faith, is always hopeful and endures through every circumstance."

I CORINTHIANS 13:7 (NLT)

"And we know that in all things, God works all things for the good of those who love him, who have been called according to his purpose."

ROMANS 8:28 (NIV)

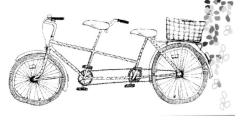

"For by him all things were created: things in heaven and on earth, visible and invisible, whether thrones or powers or rulers or authorities; all things were created by him and for him."

COLOSSIANS 1:16 (NIV)

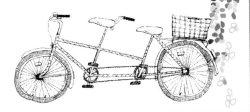

"For we are his workmanship, created in Christ Jesus for good works, which God prepared beforehand, that we should walk in them."

EPHESIANS 2:10 (ESV)

Week EIGHT: D-on't Stop Pedaling (part 2)

ICE BREAKER Questions

1. What is the worst thing your parents ever made you eat as a child?

2. If you could go back in time and change history, what would you change? Why?

JOURNAL review

STOP and take five to ten minutes to discuss your journal time. How did these Scriptures help you to ride tandem with God this week?

IT's TIME TO RIDE: Group Lesson

Today, I want to carry on the idea of tension and timing and look at two biblical characters who allowed the pain in their lives to propel them toward Jesus.

Let's read about Jairus and the bleeding woman in Luke chapter eight.

Read Luke 8:40-56.

In your own words, describe the setting of these verses?

_____

_____

What was the tension in this woman's life that led her to touch Jesus?

_____

_____

Consider the timing in this event. Where was Jesus headed when He felt the power go out of Him?

_____

_____

Why do you think this timing is significant?

_____

_____

What healed the bleeding woman?

_____

_____

What did Jesus tell Jairus about his daughter in verse 50? How would you have responded to this?

_____

_____

I find these two stories of Jesus' healing a beautiful picture of tension and timing merging into our chapter of D-on't Stop Pedaling. This is the question I ponder—What keep us from pedaling? What keeps us from believing? For the following exercise, list as many barriers you can think of that would have stopped the bleeding woman and Jairus from pedaling toward the healing power of Jesus.

The Bleeding Woman:

_____

_____

Jairus:

_____

_____

Now, it's your turn. Think of a problem, a tension in your life either past or present that keeps you from seeking Jesus. What stops you from reaching out to touch Him? What are your fears? What stops you from believing?

You:

_____

_____

_____

_____

_____

_____

I can name a few things that keep me from pedaling: Pride. Lack of time. Busyness. Unbelief. Getting other's advice first. Trusting in other's opinions. Thinking it will just go away if I ignore it. CONTROL. Wow. I don't know about you, but I just felt the Captain pull over the bike, spread out a blanket, and ask me to sit while as He does some preaching into my soul!

While tension can certainly drive us away from Jesus, it can also **propel us to pedal forward and believe in His power.** The stories of the bleeding woman and Jairus reveal to us that Jesus will stop at any moment in time, listen to our sorrows, and repair the chain. There is no judgement or condemnation. He's available and accessible. Twenty-four seven.

As we close for today, notice where Jesus was headed. _He was on the way to heal a dying child._ That's urgent, right? If you were Jesus' disciple and the ruler of the synagogue, a high standing official, came and requested you to be somewhere, my guess is that you would get there pronto! But not Jesus. He gives His listening ear to ALL His beloved children whether a high-class official or a low-class bleeding woman. He, like His Father, does not show favoritism. In His perfect timing, Jesus had TIME to stop and listen to the story of this bleeding woman and why she risked being in a crowd of Jews to reach out and touch His garment. I imagine after 12 years of bleeding, her story lasted as least 15 minutes. We will never know for sure. What we do know is that Jesus' N-ecessary Stop was long enough for Jairus' daughter to die. But again, in His perfect tension and timing, he heals Jairus' daughter and brings her back to life.

He has TIME for each of our tensions. And when we keep pedaling toward Him, there is a power (the drive chain) that drives us toward a faith to believe the impossible. We are not promised instant healing, but we are filled with a **hope** that He will always be with us. When we are up against ALL that convinces us to stop believing, I encourage you to keep pedaling—not in your own strength, but relying on the leading of the Captain to provide the power as He pedals with you. This is the beauty of a tandem bike.

Keep your feet on the pedals, don't be afraid, and believe His power is propelling you forward.

In closing, read the following verses. What do these verses tell us about God's love for us?

- **1 Corinthians 13:7**

_____
_____
_____
_____
_____

- **Ephesians 2:4-5**

_____
_____
_____
_____
_____

> "Love never gives up, never loses faith, is always hopeful and endures through every circumstance."
>
> I CORINTHIANS 13:7 (NLT)

We are alive, my friend. It's not that we were bad and made good because of Jesus. We were once dead and made ALIVE through Jesus. Looking back into these stories of surrender, belief, trust, and love, it's really not the drive train that connects the power to the back rider, it's the **grace train.** It is because of His great love for us. It is this very connection to Christ that gives us the power to overcome and be overwhelmed by His love and peace. Jesus doesn't have grease on His hands when He stops to realign our chain. No. These are blood stained hands. They are filled with grace to love us during our hardest days and deepest doubts. Do you trust in your Captain to lead you? When you feel like giving up, lean into the leading of the Commander in Chief. He has the connections! Amen.

If you are struggling with control, write a prayer using what we have learned today.

_____
_____
_____
_____
_____
_____
_____
_____
_____

I RIDE for PRAYER REQUESTS

JOURNAL QUESTIONS

* Who chose David as his servant?

* What was his job before he was chosen as King?

* How many times do you see the word sheep or shepherd in these verses?

* How did he lead the people?

God chose David to lead the people of Israel, and He took him from shepherding sheep to shepherding people. I love this transition. Don't pass by it too quickly. Four times in three verses, the 78th Psalm reminds us that God took David from the sheep pens to being the shepherd over Israel. I bet in a million years David never thought he could use his youthful days protecting sheep to being the King of Israel protecting God's children. Think about this. **God can use any gift you have for His Kingdom.**

* What skills has God blessed you with that you can use for His Kingdom?

I love that the Bible tells us "with skillful hands he led them." Simple, yet powerful. Think of a shepherd's hands.

2. What qualities do you think a shepherd needs to lead his flock?

One thing we know about sheep is that they are not very smart. They are always hungry and thirsty, and they get scared quickly. They are totally dependent on the shepherd for protection, care, food, and health. With skillful hands, the shepherd has to look ahead for potential danger, lead the flock to green pasture, still the waters so they can drink, heal their wounds, seek those that are lost, and find the ones who have strayed. I imagine there are a lot of sleepless nights and many prayers for patience and love. The words shepherd, sheep, and shepherding are used more than 250 times in the Bible. There is a reason, because again, there is a **connection.**

Jesus is our Good Shepherd. And, with skillful hands HE LEADS us, too. **It's a beautiful picture.** Think of ALL the things His hands have created. Read Colossians 1:16 in the margin.

> "For by him all things were created: things in heaven and on earth, visible and invisible, whether thrones or powers or rulers or authorities; all things were created by him and for him."
>
> COLOSSIANS 1:16

3. Look up the following verses and list ALL the wonders He has created.

• **Acts 17:24**

• **Psalm 19:1**

- **Psalm 8:3**

"When I consider your heavens, the work of your fingers, the moon and the stars, which you have set in place . . . "

- **Genesis 1:1, Genesis 1:20-21, 24, Genesis 1:27**

- **Psalm 139:13-14**

With SKILLFUL hands, God CREATED EVERYTHING. With SKILLFUL hands, God made YOU.

I believe sometimes we stop pedaling because we don't think we have anything to offer. That's baloney. You have been created by God. You are not an accident. God knit you with **purpose.** He gave you gifts and talents so you can use them to **lead** others to Him. You are chosen and you have been given the power to connect with others as you ride on this tandem journey. With skillful hands, **God made you.**

And He will **lead** you.

4. Read Ephesians 2:4-10.

* How have you been saved?

* Why can you not save yourself?

* What does God call you?

It's important to KNOW that we are made alive in Christ by grace before we can jump to the amazing reality that we are God's workmanship. Sometimes we can think we are more superior than we really are. Remember, we are lost sheep! But unlike sheep, we are created in Christ Jesus to do good works, which God prepared in advance for us to do. Again, you are no mistake. God created you KNOWING in advance that only YOU would have the certain gifts and talents you could use to bring Him glory, just like David. Pretty cool.

I met a delightful couple from Darien, Connecticut and soon learned that the grandfather's name was "**Boom.**" Yep. That's right. He was a larger man and when his grandchildren would run up to give him a big hug, they would always yell, "Boom!"

I like to think of God as my BOOM. When I run and jump into His arms, I sense the connection, the surrender, the letting go of my control, and feel the BOOM. Like a child being fully enveloped in the arms of a HUGE hug, I want this freedom to be loved unconditionally. I just want to let go and believe with unabandoned passion that He is leading me with skillful hands. The hands that formed the heavens and earth are holding me. The hands that announced the stars and gave the light to the sky gave me my passions and gifts. The hands that call in powers and authorities, call me to serve with integrity of heart. These hands made me with a plan and a purpose. BOOM.

If you are like me, sometimes you want to give up, grab the steering wheel of control, and stop pedaling altogether. Here is a **BOOM prayer** for those moments. Let's pray it together.

Dear Lord, I am a child of God, an original masterpiece. I am chosen, forgiven, and loved by the Prince of Peace. I have gifts and talents that You want me to use to lead others to You. I am a new creation. By Your love, I am righteous and redeemed. I am saved by Your love and grace alone. I am worthy and more than enough. I am called to live out my gifts and serve one another. I am loved. You are the Boom. I am the beloved. Ride on. Amen.

SOLE HOPE

Host a shoe-cutting party

—to benefit **Sole Hope**. Using your **old jeans,** you can help make shoes for kids in Uganda so they are not affected by painful jiggers. By not wearing closed-toed shoes, children and adults alike are becoming ill due to diseases (specifically a parasite called jiggers) that enter through the feet and rob the body of the little nutrition it has. Many lose their childhood to this parasite and others are unable to attend school because their feet have been so badly mutilated by jiggers.

Start PLANNING your shoe-cutting party, TODAY!

FOR MORE DETAILS
visit http://solehopeparty.org/
home-parties-planner/

Week NINE: Enjoy the Ride

1. What crazy activities do you dream of trying someday?

2. What was one new experience you tried that was completely unknown or uncomfortable to you at the time you tried it?

JOURNAL review

STOP and take five to ten minutes to discuss your journal time. How did these Scriptures help you to ride tandem with God this week?

IT's TIME TO RIDE: Group Lesson

Week five is about E-njoying the Ride.

I love that while I am writing this Bible study, God is teaching me volumes about Riding Tandem with Him. E-njoying the Ride is about maintaining a JOY-filled spirit as we ride with God in this tandem journey. This week we will discover how our fruit allows us to enJOY the present moment— even when life is not going the direction we intend. E-njoying the Ride will take **complete surrender** and trust as we follow the leader; especially when our lives seem to be racing at ninety miles to nothing. We will learn that a key to enjoying the ride is to have a **heart of praise**. We will also learn that laughter is a good thing! Our Captain is creative and not always serious. He offers hope and is the provider of **all** our enjoyment.

E-njoying the Ride is essential to our tandem journey. Let's get started!

We are going to start our week by reading Numbers 14:1-9.

To give you some background, we see the Israelites complaining **again** that their days in Egypt were more glorious than their current situation in the desert (Numbers 14:1-4). We have already learned that a complaining heart tends to exaggerate our circumstances, but here we see it can also *steal our joy.* In the previous chapter (Numbers 13), Joshua, Caleb, and 10 other men were sent on a mission to spy out the promised land God was going to give them. Their job was to investigate and ask questions like: What kind of land was it? Who lived there? What kind of soil did it have? What about the trees? When they returned, they gave a **great** report on the land. They even brought back a sample of the fruit. While Caleb was gung-ho to take possession, the other men spread a bad report that the people of the land were too gigantic to conquer. Fear struck and the Israelites were paralyzed to move forward.

Describe the fear of the people going into the promised land. (Numbers 14:3)

_____

_____

_____

How do Caleb and Joshua try to convince the people that going is good?

_____

_____

What is the Lord's promise to the Israelites if they choose to follow His lead?

_____

_____

_____

What is Joshua and Caleb's warning to the people? (Numbers 14:9)

_____

_____

_____

You might be thinking, why on earth are we studying this passage on our first day of E-njoying the Ride? Here's why. In order to experience the JOY of the Lord in the present moment, we have to FIRST learn to **follow** where He leads. We cannot rebel and do our own thing. We cannot allow the fear of our circumstances to override the confidence in our Captain. We cannot let what we **see** (or think we see) steal our joy and our assurance that God is our leader. He is WITH us. Caleb and Joshua were sent ahead to scout out the land, and they came back with fruit. GOOD fruit—solid proof that the land they were to conquer was a **future blessing**.

For a fun exercise, let's look at what fruit represents in Scripture.

Look up all or some of the following verses. In each verse, identify the fruit and write down why good fruit will allow you to E-njoy the Ride?

• **Psalm 128:1-4**

_____/_____

_____

• **Gal. 5:22-23**

_____/_____

_____

• **Proverbs 12:14**

_____/_____

_____

• **Proverbs 11:30**

_____/_____

_____

• **Hosea 10:12**

"I said, 'Plant the good seeds of righteousness, and you will harvest a crop of love. Plow up the hard ground of your hearts, for now is the time to seek the LORD, that he may come and shower righteousness upon you.'"
HOSEA 10:12 NEW LIVING TRANSLATION

_____/_____

_____

- **Matthew 12:33-35.**

_____/_____

_____

Our fruit can be our attitude, our words, our work, our actions, our praise, our worship, and our thanksgiving. Our fruit represents what is in our heart. To be able to E-njoy the Ride, the fruit has to be good in our hearts. Fruit can go either way. It can be fresh or as rotten as the bad influence of the unbelieving spies. Because of their fear, the Israelites didn't believe in Joshua and Caleb's report. They also wanted to stone Moses and Aaron and initiate new leadership. Lesson to learn: We will follow the wrong leader when we have bad fruit in our hearts. When we sow the promises of Scripture into our hearts, we can E-njoy the Ride because we are confident that our Captain is with us. He is leading us into good land even when there is fear or uncertainty. You cannot enjoy the ride when there is bad fruit spoiling the basket of your circumstance. Don't allow the appearance of your surroundings to scare you from the promises of God. **The fruit from the Promise Land is always good.**

Have you ever been scared to step into something new because you were afraid?

_____

_____

_____

_____

God's purpose for your life has purpose! God doesn't want us to be afraid, He wants us to Enjoy this Ride because He knows the plans ahead.

Choose one of the following verses to look up. What do the following verses say about how we are to plan our steps?

- **Proverbs 16:9, Proverbs 19:21, or Psalm 37:23-24**

_____

_____

_____

The word for *establish* in Proverbs 16:9 and *makes firm* in Psalm 37:23 is *kuwn* which means to set up, to be firm, to be established, be prepared.[11] The word for *prevails* in Proverbs 19:21 is *quwm* which also means to establish, to stand, to set.[12]

It is clear to me that you are not a cosmic mistake. God did not haphazardly make you one day on His lunch break. No. God set your plans into motion and established them with purpose. When bumps hit here and there, they do not take God by surprise. God is fully aware and prepared for everything we encounter. We can learn to E-njoy the Ride during the good times and the bad times by holding on and LEANING into the One who is LEADING.

I RIDE *for* PRAYER REQUESTS

1. Read what Mark Batterson says in Draw the Circle, The 40-Day Prayer Challenge.

"God wants us to get where God wants us to go more than we want to get where God wants us to go. Follow the script of the Holy Scripture and the improvisation of the Holy Spirit."[13]

You might have to read that again. Slowly. It's too good to miss. I love this quote because it reminds me of my modern dance teacher, Diann Catlin. As a warm-up for class, she would have us dance "improvisations." She would tell us to dance like we are a piece of gum stuck to the bottom of a shoe, or a car shifting gears, or a hurricane, a flower opening, or a kitchen disposal. You name it, we probably danced it. I loved improvisations! Here we are reminded that God has already established our steps. To E-njoy the Ride, we are called to imitate Him and dance with abandon to the tune of the **Holy Spirit.**

* What do these verses tell us about Scripture and following the Holy Spirit?

- **Deuteronomy 5:1**

- **Exodus 18:20**

- **Psalm 32:8**

- **Ephesians 5:1-2**

Learning Scripture is like learning the choreography to a beautiful dance. We are to imitate the moves of the Teacher and watch the way He dances. This takes time and discipline. We can't just step out on the stage of life without knowing, learning, listening to, and watching the Master Choreographer. We have to **practice** so that when we are called to dance, we know the steps. In ballet, we are told to dance "full-out." I think this can apply to our lives, as well. Because we have placed full trust in the choreography, we can dance FULL OUT and E-njoy the Ride. We don't even have to worry about forgetting the steps as long as we are following the script of the Scriptures. The Holy Spirit will remind us of the dance just when we need it. The steps are choreographed with an established purpose and inspired with passion and love.

2. How are you going to dance "full out" today?

* Write a prayer to the Master Choreographer who knows our steps. I'll start us off.

Dear Jesus, thank You for being our Master Choreographer! You have established our steps with purpose. You have gone before us to prepare the way so that we don't have to worry about what is ahead. You are in charge of the choreography. Our job is to learn the steps of Scripture so we can dance FULL OUT with passion and love. I pray our dance would inspire and touch the lives of others so they, too, will want to know the Maker of our dance.

When I sit down and think about E-njoying this tandem Ride with God, why is it that my mind tends to go to the things I have to do or better yet, haven't done? Are you like me?

3. How do we E-njoy this tandem Ride with God when our lives are so busy?

Life seems to take over and go by at such a fast pace that it doesn't seem possible to stop and E-njoy the Ride. How do we do this? We have seen how mountainous obstacles can steal our joy and our fruit. We have also learned how Scripture guides us to dance the steps God has established and planned out for us. But, honestly, how do we E-njoy the Ride we are on?

Let's look at **surrender.** At first, this word might not look like a fun tandem bike experience, but I promise, it will be the best ride you will ever take!

For the full context of reading, read Joshua 3:1-17. We will be focusing on verse Joshua 3:5.

* What does God tell the people to do today to prepare for tomorrow? Why do you think this would be significant in our learning to E-njoying the Ride with God?

The word for **sanctify** can mean to purify, to be set apart, to consecrate.[14] Google tells us that the word for **consecrate** means to dedicate formally to a divine purpose. What I hear God telling us is this: You cannot be about your own purposes and God's promises at the same time. You need to surrender your agenda because it **competes with God's agenda.** It is like oil and water. I hear God saying loud and clear that in order to E-njoy the Ride, we need to SURRENDER our control! This means no hands on the handlebars girls! Check out the promise. If we sanctify, or set apart our lives, and learn the choreography of Scripture **today,** then **tomorrow** we will see the wonders of God! The word for wonder in Joshua 3:5 is the same word for wonderful in Psalm 119:18:

"Open my eyes that I may see wonderful things in your law."

Do you remember what wonderful means? It is the things that we, in and of ourselves, cannot do on our own. It is the surpassing, the marvelous, the beyond's one power, the too difficult to understand. God will show Himself wonderful if we consecrate ourselves today.

4. What are you going through that seems difficult to understand? How will you open your eyes to see that God could be doing a wonderful thing in your life?

This passage in Joshua describes the **wonderful things** God was about to do for the people of Israel. They had served their sentence in the desert for 40 years and now, God was giving them a second chance to enter the promised land through the leadership of Joshua. This time they were not scared of giants. They did not retreat back into their own plans. Instead, they were COMPLETELY SURRENDERED to step into the Jordan at flood stage. As soon as their feet touched the water, the river dried up and they were able to cross on dry land! I call that a WONDER—a miracle that only God could have done. The Israelites fully surrendered their lives into the promises of God and were about **to dance** into the promised land.

5. What do the following verses tell us about how God's faithfulness will never leave us as we dance into His promises?

- **Isaiah 52:12**

"You will not leave in a hurry, running for your lives. For the LORD will go ahead of you; yes, the God of Israel will protect you from behind." Isaiah 52:12 (NLT)

- **Exodus 13:21**

- **Exodus 14:13**

- **How will you apply this to your life today?**

I have friends who don't want to believe in Jesus because they feel they will lose their independence. They associate losing control with trusting in Jesus. Nothing could be further from the truth. The more we grip onto the "I'm-going-to-do-this-my-way" attitude, the further we backtrack into the desert and away from the promised land. I believe that in order to E-njoy the Ride, we have to stop trying to steer the handlebars from the back. They don't move, and they will never steer no matter how hard we try. Remember our lesson in N-ecessary Stops? By taking the first small steps of faith to believe, our eyes will be open to see the wonderful things of God. We have to **believe first** in order for us to **see** the promises of God. These verses above are a fresh reminder that God goes ahead of us and guides us. He is our Good Shepherd. We do not have to be afraid. We do not have to be in a hurry as though we are running for our lives. We don't have to be awakened by our "to-do" lists and jump out of bed to speed into our day. Did you catch what Exodus 14:13 tells us to do in order to E-njoy the Ride? We have to **stand still.** We have to be still in order to WATCH God in our lives.

* Take a look at these two words: STAND and STILL. How do you think the strength of these words together will allow you to E-njoy the Ride? Why not just stand? Why not just be still? Why is their more power when they Ride Tandem together?

In order for us to E-njoy the Ride we have to STAND on the foundation of Scripture and sit still while God directs our purposeful paths. It's not always easy to surrender the front seat, but the ride is so much better. As much as we want to be in control, we need to fully consecrate and surrender to the ride God is taking us on. Trust Him, let go of the back handlebars, and feel the breeze as you E-njoy the Ride! Read this sweet message from *Streams in the Desert*:

"Sit still, my daughter, just sit calmly still. What higher service could you for Him fill? It's hard! Ah, yes! But choicest things must cost! For lack of losing and how much is lost! It's hard, it's true! But then He gives you grace to count the hardest spot the sweetest place."
J. Danson Smith[15]

If you think you are losing the race by taking the time to sit still, I am here to encourage you today! You are actually winning the race because you are surrendering your agenda to the God who has your life in the palm of His hand.

* In closing, write down the specific things you are going to surrender today to the One who knows how hard it is to give up control.

Jesus knows. He died on the cross for you and for me. Even Jesus let His Father have the front seat. Because He did, **we** can E-njoy the Ride. Because of His SURRENDER, we can SEE the wonderful things the Lord has for us. Consecrate yourselves and sit today so you can WATCH for all the amazing things God will do tomorrow!

Week TEN: Enjoy the Ride (part two)

ICE BREAKER Questions

I break for ICE BREAKERS

1. What was the best thing that happened to you this past week?

2. If given a chance, which person would you like to be for a day? Or who would you like to exchange roles with?

JOURNAL review

STOP and take five to ten minutes to discuss your journal time. How did these Scriptures help you to ride tandem with God this week?

IT's TIME TO RIDE: Group Lesson

I hope you feel a little lighter this morning as you surrender more and more control over to the One who is steering your tandem journey!

I can't wait to SEE what God will show you in your life today because you surrendered yesterday! Keep watch! Keep your eyes OPEN and look for the mighty hand of God.

Today, we are going to look how PRAISE allows us to E-njoy the Ride! Instead of looking at all the things that are going wrong, let's praise God for all that is **going right!** I love this prayer I wrote in my journal. I hope it will encourage you, too!

Today Lord, I choose to hop on the back seat of the tandem and let You steer. Where are You taking me today, Lord? Yes, I will pedal, and yes, I will trust. While I can't see the road ahead, I believe You can. You have gone before me and because I have spent time in Your Word, I am prepared to ride with You today. I am equipped because You are my lead. You are my guide. There may be times when I am afraid and clutch a little too tightly to my handlebars, but I know You will never leave Your seat as Captain of my life. I may want You to pedal faster to speed things up. I may ask You to slow things down, or perhaps stop, so I can catch my breath. I know You've got this Lord, and You have my best interest in Your heart. We are a team as we Ride Tandem together. With You as my Captain, we will win this race. We will press on together until the finish line. Steady my bike, sweet Lord, so that I may climb on. Balance the bike for me so I can take my position on the back. I am your co-pilot. Lead me into the way everlasting. Amen.

Today, let's celebrate the ride of our LIVES and give the Captain some **praise**. He's got this. It does not matter how big or little your circumstances are, He knows the road ahead. Let's not look at what's going wrong, but rather shift our eyes on ALL that's going **right.** Today, focus on ALL that He has done for YOU and shout out some PRAISE!

Look up the following verses and write down all the reasons you can E-njoy the Ride!

- **Psalm 118:24**

"This is the day that the LORD has made; let us rejoice and be glad in it." Psalm 118:24

_____
_____
_____

- **Psalm 95:1-7**

_____
_____
_____

- **Proverbs 31:25**

_____
_____
_____

- **Psalm 65:1-8**

_____
_____
_____

These are just a few verses that give us a reason to E-njoy the Ride! Our God is simply amazing. Do you forget this at times? I know that when my life feels overwhelming, I seem to forget who GOD IS. Instead of focusing on the problem, we need to shout out some PRAISE. Come, let us sing for JOY to the Lord! He has created everything we look at every day. That alone should get our hearts excited to rejoice! We are to PRAISE the One who gave us laughter. Don't take life too seriously. We are clothed with strength and dignity. We CAN laugh at the days to come when we are seated in the back trusting in the Captain. Jesus experienced everything you and I encounter, but too often, I tend to focus on His suffering. What about ALL His creativity, fun, and LAUGHTER? I bet He had some good times with His disciples. Don't you think? You just know they were laughing when that fish had coins in his mouth. What?

Read Matthew 17:24-27.

What happens in this story that is super creative? How can we rejoice in Jesus' fun side?

_____

_____

_____

The point of reading this story is not to decide who is or who is not exempt from paying the King's taxes. What I want you to notice is how creative and fun Jesus is! He could have paid this tax in so many ways. But He decides to use a fish with the exact money in his mouth to teach His disciples to trust Him in ALL things! How WONDERful is this lesson!

I asked you in your journal time to write down the things you were going to surrender to God in order for Him to show you His wonders. Today, I want you to write down the WONDERS that God has shown you. Once you have written the wonders, write a PRAISE next to them! The ride is getting exciting! Doesn't it feel good to rejoice?

• Wonders	• Praise
_____ /	_____
_____ /	_____
_____ /	_____
_____ /	_____
_____ /	_____
_____ /	_____
_____ /	_____
_____ /	_____

I want to end today with Psalm 100—a Psalm of thanksgiving from God's Word Translation.

> "Shout happily to the LORD, all the earth. Serve the LORD cheerfully. Come into his presence with a joyful song. Realize that the LORD alone is God. He made us, and we are his. We are his people and the sheep in his care. Enter his gates with a song of thanksgiving. Come into his courtyards with a song of praise. Give thanks to him; praise his name. The LORD is good. His mercy endures forever. His faithfulness endures throughout every generation." PSALM 100 (GW)

Look at all the action verbs in this verse! I've gone ahead and written them down. Now write how you will apply them to your lives specifically.

SHOUT happily to the Lord. _____
_____
_____

SERVE the Lord cheerfully. _____
_____
_____

COME into His presence with a joyful song. _____
_____
_____

REALIZE that the LORD alone is God. _____
_____
_____

ENTER His gates with a song of thanksgiving. _____
_____
_____

COME into his courtyards with a song of praise. ____
_____
_____

GIVE thanks to Him. _____

_____

_____

PRAISE His name. _____

_____

_____

To E-njoy this Ride, we must rejoice! When we greet God in the morning, shout out His name and thank Him for all the goodness in your life. Why? Because He is GOOD, and His love endures forever. And ever. And ever. Forevermore. Have you ever noticed the **more** on forever? That is a LONG bike ride my friend! Lets learn to E-njoy the Ride on this side of the abundant life that Christ offers.

As we close for today, just write God a prayer telling Him all you have learned in your journey of Riding Tandem so far.

_____

_____

_____

_____

_____

_____

_____

_____

_____

_____

_____

_____

_____

_____

_____

_____

_____

_____

I RIDE
for PRAYER
REQUESTS

I hope you have discovered that we need to worry less and praise more! I want to start out our journal time today by reading this quote from Sarah Young in *Jesus Calling*:

> "Learn to enjoy life more. Relax. Remembering that I am God with you. I crafted you with enormous capacity to know Me and to ENJOY my presence." [16]

One of the ways I believe God crafts us with the capacity to know Him is by **using our stories to tandem with the truths of Scripture.** As a speaker, I have always been taught to weave in personal stories to make God's Word more applicable. This truth is not only for speakers, but also for every one of us. If you think about it, the entire Bible contains stories of men and women whose lives were touched by the truth of Scripture. It's our turn now. We need to weave our stories into Scripture and tell others of God's amazing grace! When we understand the Bible in a more personal way, I believe God becomes real. E-njoying the Ride is allowing God to use our stories to teach us the truth of His Word.

This past summer, Daley and her friend Adam were hiking in the Smoky Mountains. When they got to the top of their hike, they decided to take a path down that was not well traveled. About an hour into the trip, they both decided they were **lost.** With little cell phone reception, Adam managed to call his Mom, Kellie. Adam told her the situation but couldn't tell her their location. When Kellie got to the parking lot to hike up the mountain to find them, she ran into a couple that was about to hike up this exact trail. Kellie told them her concern and without hesitation the man went to his trunk, grabbed his hiking vest, three water bottles, a compass, a knife (to bushwhack if necessary), and took off.

Kellie was a little stunned and asked his wife if this was a normal response. "Yes," she responded. "He is a retired Navy Seal. It's what he does. It's how he **serves. He will find them.**" When the kind woman exchanged phone numbers with Kellie, the man's wife opened her phone with a password. Do you know what it was? TRUST IN GOD. Amazing, right?

This story not only allowed me to trust God more, but showed Kellie to trust more, and most definitely Daley and Adam to **trust more.** God showed Himself in a very real and tangible way that day!

1. Now it's your turn! Describe a time in your life when you saw God working in a tangible way?

2. Let's look at a story in Scripture that might resonate in our hearts the same way.

* Let's read Luke 15:1-7. What did the shepherd do when he learned one of his sheep was missing? How did the shepherd celebrate when he found the lost sheep?

* How does Jesus use this story to "tandem" the truth that all heaven celebrates when one lost soul is found?

When Daley told me the story of how they were lost and then found, **I celebrated!** When I learned that a retired Navy Seal left his wife and Kellie in the parking lot to hike up the mountain to find Daley and Adam, my mind triggered to the story of the lost sheep. Mr. Navy Seal, just like the shepherd, was not going to stop until they were found. Jesus didn't stop either. **It's who He is. It's how He serves.** He sacrificed everything so that we could be found and saved. He sacrificed His life so we could make it to the party of salvation and eternal life. That's a day of rejoicing!

Why should we E-njoy the Ride? Because there is a lot of **rejoicing** to be done!

3. Look at the following verses. Find the word ENJOY and write down why we should be joyful.

• **Deuteronomy 6:1-2**

• **Psalm 37:3-4**

• **Ephesians 6:1-3**

• **1 Timothy 6:17**

We get to ENJOY a long life when we follow the ways of the Lord. When we TRUST in Him and do good, we will ENJOY safe pasture. When we obey our parents, we will ENJOY a long life on this earth. We need to put our hope in God and not in wealth, which is so uncertain, because God is the only ONE who can provide for our true enJOYment. I love how the New Living Translation reads:

> "Teach those who are rich in this world not to be proud and not to trust in their money, which is so unreliable. Their trust should be in God, who richly gives us all we need for our enjoyment." TIMOTHY 6:17 (NLT)

Do you catch that? I have been saving this verse for last because this is the very reason we can E-njoy the Ride! GOD is the ONLY ONE who can provide the enJOYment! If this statement is true, which I wholeheartedly believe it is, then why do we not enjoy **all** that God has provided? The reason is this: We focus on what we don't have and miss out on what we DO HAVE. What a JOY killer.

4. What in your life do you focus on that takes your attention away from God? How can you change this?

I find myself in this place too often. Put on the brakes. Stop the bike. Look at your positioning. Chances are, my friend, you are in the wrong seat and dancing to the wrong song. Your fruit has become sour, and you are not completely surrendered to the direction of your Captain. Climb on the back and lean into the leading of God. He has given you **everything you need.** Relax and remember His goodness.

5. As we close for the week, write down all the things God has placed in your life for you to E-njoy the Ride. Be creative. This is a FUN ride!

WOW. What a week! I hope you needed another piece of paper to write down all that God has given you to enjoy this incredible life. No mountain is too high, and no valley is too deep for God to pour out His love on His children. God is always with us and will never leave us. As we close with prayer, let us always remember that our Lord is the only ONE who richly gives us all that we NEED for us to E-njoy the Ride. Great job.

Thank you, Lord, for all You have shown us this week about E-njoying the Ride. We have so much to be thankful for. Teach us to trust in You no matter the enormity of our circumstance. Please do not allow the fear of the unknown to override our confidence in You. You have made us with purpose as we dance to Your choreography. Help us to surrender today so we can SEE Your wonders tomorrow. We need to stand still to fulfill the purposes You have set before us. May we always rejoice and praise You for all we have been given. Thank You, Lord, that You never give up on us, but keep looking for us when we lose our way. Continue to use our stories to deepen our relationship with You. Help us to show others how amazing You are. I pray we would E-njoy this tandem Ride because only You can fulfil our heart's deepest desires. Only with You can we E-njoy this Ride. Lead us, Lord, and teach us to lean into Your leading. Amen.

"Let the morning bring me word of
your unfailing love, for I have
put my trust in you. Show me the
way I should go, for to you
I entrust my life."

PSALM 143:8 (NIV)

"Therefore be imitators of God,
as beloved children. And walk in
love, as Christ loved us and gave
himself up for us, a fragrant
offering and sacrifice to God."

EPHESIANS 5:1-2 (NIV)

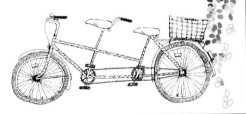

"Shout happily to the LORD, all the
earth. Serve the LORD cheerfully.
Come into his presence with a joyful
song. Realize that the LORD alone
is God. He made us, and we are his.
We are his people and the sheep in
his care. Enter his gates with a
song of thanksgiving. Come into his
courtyards with a song of praise.
Give thanks to him; praise his name."

PSALM 100:1-6 (GW))

MEMORY cards

Week ELEVEN: MARK THE MOMENTS

1. What do you consider the most important event of your life so far?

2. Describe a real-life situation where you stood up for someone or something.

JOURNAL review

STOP and take five to ten minutes to discuss your journal time. How did these Scriptures help you to ride tandem with God this week?

IT's TIME TO RIDE: Group Lesson

This is our last concept in Riding Tandem and it's time to M-ark the Moment! But, this will not be our last stop.

Riding Tandem with the Lord means that we get to ride on, and on, and on . . . until the promised finish line where we will see Jesus face to face. Remember, this ride is only the beginning. **Eternity is forever.** He leads us into everlasting life. This is the **hope** that allows us to M-ark the Moment. Any moment.

As a refresher, lets look again at Riding T. A. N. D. E. M. Let's begin with T-ime for Takeoff and the importance of A-ligning ourselves with the direction of our Captain.

- **T-ime for Takeoff**
- **A-lignment**

Let's review Psalm 139:23-24.

> "Search me, God, and know my heart; test me and know my anxious thoughts. See if there is any offensive way in me, and lead me in the way everlasting." Psalm 139:23-24

Why would these verses be important for T-ime for Takeoff? What about A-lignment?

_____

_____

_____

_____

_____

_____

Before we ride with God in the morning (T-ime for Takeoff), it is imperative that we pray Psalm 139:23-24. Remember, in order to **see** the Lord work amazing things, we need to consecrate ourselves **today**. We need to ask the Lord each morning to search us, test us, and examine our hearts to see if there is anything that will throw us off balance (A-lignment). The tendency for busy girls (me included) is to hop on the front and start pedaling. But, too often we find ourselves pedaling from the front seat, gripping the handlebars of control while dragging all the extra weight behind. Do you remember what the instruction manual says from lesson one? The Captain has a reason for the tandem seating arrangement. He knows we can't steer AND pedal. Only He can. With God in the driver's seat, we can climb to heights we never thought possible.

- **N-ecessary Stops**
- **D-on't Stop Pedaling**

Let's review Matthew 11:28-30 and look at N-ecessary Stops and D-on't Stop Pedaling.

> "Come to me, all you who are weary and burdened, and I will give you rest. Take my yoke upon you and learn from me, for I am gentle and humble in heart, and you will find rest for your souls. For my yoke is easy and my burden is light." Matthew 11:28-30

In light of Riding Tandem, how is Jesus encouraging us to take N-ecessary Stops and D-on't Stop Pedaling?

_____

_____

_____

_____

_____

_____

_____

Jesus is telling us, "Come to me. I've got this! Don't rely on your own strength. If you keep pedaling in your own power, you will become weary and burdened. Take **N-ecessary Stops** and sit for a while. I can and will give you rest, rest for your soul. **D-on't Stop Pedaling**. Don't give up and learn from Me along the way. I am unlike the world that tells you to pedal faster and harder just to be noticed and valued. I love you just the way you are. Even in the fast pace of life, you can **E-njoy this Ride** because I am with you. I will be your strength, and I will never leave you to ride alone. Never. I am gentle. I am humble. I am here."

Come with me on this tandem journey.

- **E-njoy the Ride**

We need to **E-njoy the Ride** God has for **us**. Just as every bike is different, God has designed each of us with a different purpose, passion, and provision. He will supply our every need, and we do not have to worry about the road ahead. We see this truth in Paul's tandem ride with Jesus.

Let's review and read Philippians 4:15-20, with a focus on Philippians 4:19.

What do you think it means that we are supplied with ALL of our needs through Jesus Christ?

_____

_____

_____

_____

While Paul is thanking the church in Philipi for contributing to his earthly needs, this verse (Philippians 4:19) shows us Paul's confidence in God to supply EVERY NEED as well—earthly and spiritual. God will never leave us without His provision. The same glorious riches the Father gave to His Son, Jesus, He gives to us as well. We can **E-njoy this Ride** because we are **completely** taken care of. In order to believe this and find rest for our souls, we need to:

- Take intentional **T-ime for Takeoff**
- **A-lign** ourselves with the Lord
- Know the **N-ecessary Stopping** points
- **D-on't Stop Pedaling** when life gets hard
- **E-njoy and Ride** and press on

Do you see how fascinating the concept is of Riding Tandem with the Lord? My prayer is that even when you finish this study, you will always be reminded of this simple acronym—T. A. N. D. E. M.

Now it's time to learn about **M-ark the Moment**—our final "hurrah" where we can celebrate ALL that God has shown us in this amazing study! To begin this week, I am going to share with you one of my favorite M-ark the Moments in Scripture. It's the foundation of my ministry ThouArtExalted (1 Corinthians 29:11, KJV).

`Lets read together 1 Chronicles 29:1-20 (It's long but totally worth reading!)`

What is the task at hand, and for whom is the temple being built? (1 Chronicles 29:1)

_____

_____

_____

Who has provided for the construction of the temple? (1 Chronicles 29:2-5)

_____

_____

Why is David so overwhelmed with joy? (1 Chronicles 29:6-9)

_____

_____

What does David call the Lord in his prayer of overwhelming joy? (1 Chronicles 29:10-13)

_____

_____

_____

How do you see David's humility? (1 Chronicles 29:14-16)

_____

_____

From where does our provision come? (1 Chronicles 29:14)

_____

_____

What happens when the people are so willing to give back to the Lord?

_____

_____

These verses are the pinnacle of **M-ark the Moment!** We see ALL the steps of Riding Tandem in David's actions. We see his taking the **T-ime for Takeoff** in the previous chapter, 1 Chronicles 28, where he understood his role in the building of the temple. David wanted to build it, but because he was a "warrior and had shed blood," the job was designed for his son, Solomon. Instead of having a pity-party, David **A-ligned** himself with the will of God and took action to prepare Solomon's heart to wholeheartedly follow after the Lord (1 Chronicles 28:9-10). David took the **N-ecessary Stops** to give Solomon all the plans the Holy Spirit had given him down to the very last detail (1 Chronicles 28:11-19). David **Never Stopped Pedaling** as he not only gave out of his personal treasures to build the temple, but also appealed to the people to give from their hearts. We arrive at the highlight of the event where ALL the people of Israel are **E-njoying the Ride** because of their overflowing love and generosity. We can **M-ark this Moment** in history because ALL was provided to build the temple, and God alone was glorified! WOW.

Did you notice David's question in 1 Chronicles 29:5?

`"Now, who is willing to consecrate themselves to the LORD today?"`
`1 Chronicles 29:5`

Now, who is willing to consecrate himself today to the Lord? Why is this amazing? Because this is the same word we looked at last week—**consecrate.**

`Joshua told the people, "Consecrate yourselves, for tomorrow the`
`LORD will do amazing things among you." Joshua 1:5`

Consecrate. Purify. Set yourselves apart for the Lord. Get on the back of the tandem (I am sure that's what consecrate means in Hebrew!) for tomorrow you will see His wonders! Yes. I love when we get to **see** (uncover, reveal) a golden thread through Scripture.

I hope you are getting the idea of what it means to M-ark the Moment. It's the perfect way to end our ride together rejoicing in ALL that God did and continues to do for us—in the small moments where no one is watching, as well as the BIG moments for all to see. All week, we will be looking at marking moments where we can **see** the acronym of Riding Tandem and the hand of God—both from our lives and Scripture. Its going to be so exciting!

`M-ark the Moments show us the incredible joy and`
`generosity when we believe ALL we have is from God and`
`for God.`

I RIDE
for PRAYER
REQUESTS

When we live in the mindset of E-njoying this tandem Ride and **M-arking the special Moments, we will see** God show Himself to us in personal ways.

Two years ago, my daughter Daley worked at Crooked Creek, a Young Life camp in Colorado. She was on summer wait staff where she served over 800 campers three meals a day. While she had to get up e-a-r-l-y to set up for breakfast, Daley's leaders also made it a priority for them to have a quiet time before they rode through their day. She e-mailed me in delight with this passage from Luke 4:40.

"Mom," she said, "I can bring my heart, my experiences, and my disappointments all to Jesus and **one-by-one,** He can heal me, too."

This was not only a moment marker for Daley, but also for me. When I pray for my children's faith, I pray for them to know Jesus intimately. Daley, at 15, had discovered Jesus in a personal way. It wasn't my faith, her dad's faith, her friends' faith, but hers alone. She was taking the time to prepare her heart (T-ime for Takeoff) and allowing the Captain to steady her bike (A-lignment). She was learning to take stops when needed (N-ecessary Stops) and keep pressing on through long days (D-on't Stop Pedaling). She was E-njoying the Ride because she was seeing firsthand how Scripture can tandem with personal experience. Daley was allowing her stories to intertwine with the Word that is holy and true. The result? An authentic faith that **propels more trust** to believe, and love, and give, and serve, and tell others about the Captain of her life—ALL with a thankful heart. She was **M-arking the Moment** and mine, too.

> "When the sun was setting, the people brought to Jesus all who had various kinds of sickness, and laying his hands on each one, he healed them."
>
> LUKE 4:40

1. Let's look at a passage in Scripture where another woman's faith becomes personal. Read John 4:4-26.

* What initial question did Jesus ask the Samaritan woman? (John 4:7)

* What was her answer? (John 4:9)

* What did Jesus know about this woman? Did it stop Him from telling her the truth? (John 4:18)

* At what point in the story do you think the Samaritan woman had a M-arking Moment?

2. Read John 4:27-42.

* What happened because of this woman's belief in Jesus?

* How did she give M-arking Moments to others in the town? How did their faith become personal, like Daley's? (John 4:42)

I'm curious to see where you put the Samaritan's M-ark the Moment turnaround. Was it when Jesus revealed her past? Was it when Jesus declared He was the Messiah? I'm sure the whole day was a M-ark the Moment in and of itself, but I believe her moment was the initial **invitation** to get Him some water. Jesus, a man and a Jew, should never have been talking to a woman in the first place, let alone a Samaritan with a not-so-good reputation. He met her in her everyday world and invited her into His Kingdom. Her gender, her class, or how many times she had been married did not matter. Jesus loved her as He loves us—**abundantly** and without judgement. We are ALL His children, and we are ALL invited to ride one-on-one with the King of all Kings. This invitation was the opening of a new life, a new ride, and a chance to be forgiven and leave the past behind. Jesus did not sugar coat her current situation, but He extended her grace.

3. Let's read 2 Corinthians 5:14-21.

* How is it possible that you are a new creation in Christ?

* What do you think is the ministry of reconciliation?

* What are we called in 2 Corinthians 5:20?

The word for reconcile is to settle an account. Jesus settled the account of sin once and for all. We are all invited to be new creations in Christ. I like to call it the **New Creation Invitation!** I can remember my invitation like it was yesterday. Jesus met me, too, in a very low spot. He invited me to be a new creation, to understand my need for forgiveness, and to believe for all eternity that I can Ride Tandem with Him! He settled my sin account on the cross, and He settled yours, too. I love what the Samaritan woman did in response to her invitation. She **hurried** to the village to tell everyone about this man! The word spread and many came to believe that day.

An invitation to believe in Him leads to intimacy. Intimacy leads to tandem riding, and tandem riding leads to telling others **your story. Your testimony. Your M-ark the Moments.** Have you ever considered that your story could become someone else's invitation to know Jesus? As tandem riders, it is our mission to live the gospel and **hurry** to share the gospel. We are called to know Him and then to make Him known. The Samaritan woman made Him known that day.

Funny. As I type this, my Apple computer keeps inviting me to upgrade to the newest software. Do you know what it is called?

El Capitan. (Yes, it's spelled right.) This reminds me that once we have accepted the initial invitation to ride with Jesus, He invites us everyday to upgrade our journey with Him. Upgrade our thoughts. Upgrade our praise. Upgrade our vision. Upgrade our actions. Upgrade our compassion. Upgrade our trust. Upgrade our passion to share Jesus with others.

Let's close our journal section with 2 Corinthians 5:14-15 explaining why we long to tell others of our M-ark the Moments.

"For Christ's love compels us, because we are convinced that one died for all, and therefore all died. And he died for all, that those who live should no longer live for themselves but for him who died for them and was raised again" 2 CORINTHIANS 5:14-15

* Are you compelled by Christ's love? How are you convinced that Jesus died once and for all for your sin?

* What areas in your life do you need to upgrade to El Capitan?

It's **never** too late. Luke 4:40 tells us that while the sun was setting, Jesus laid His hands on them and healed them **one-by-one**. It doesn't matter where you are on your journey, as long as you receive, open, and RSVP to the invitation. Yes, Lord. I accept with pleasure your kind invitation to make me a new creation! What a special day. Thank you for your honesty. Jesus will meet you right where you are hurting and need some upgrading.

In a closing prayer, write down your M-ark the Moment when you received your New Creation Invitation. We need to remember this great moment so we can share our story with others. Amen.

"Search me, God, and know my heart; test me and know my anxious thoughts. See if there is any offensive way in me, and lead me in the way everlasting."

PSLAM 139:23-24 (NIV)

"Come to me, all you who are weary and burdened, and I will give you rest. Take my yoke upon you and learn from me, for I am gentle and humble in heart, and you will find rest for your souls. For my yoke is easy and my burden is light."

MATTHEW 11:28-30 (NIV)

"Thine, O Lord is the greatness, and the power, and the glory, and the victory, and the majesty: for all that is in the heaven and in the earth is thine; thine is the kingdom, O Lord, and THOU ART EXALTED as head above all."

I CHRONICLES 29:11 (KJV)

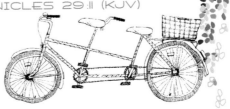

ICE BREAKER Questions

1. What do you think is the greatest invention in your lifetime and why?

2 What is the most beautiful thing you have ever seen in nature?

JOURNAL review

STOP and take five to ten minutes to discuss your journal time. How did these Scriptures help you to ride tandem with God this week?

IT's TIME TO RIDE: Group Lesson

I love that we get to close our study with M-ark the Moments. It's almost as if we are closing with a journal of our journey together.

Today, we get to peek inside a story of sincerity and hope and trust and belief in the one and only Lord. It is a prayer that illustrates the sweetness of Riding Tandem. It is the journey of Mary, the mother of our Lord Jesus.

Read Luke 1:26-56.

Let's be creative today! I want you to identify where Mary rode tandem with the Lord's plans for her life. There are no right or wrong answers (or grading for that matter!). You don't have to go in order either. Have fun with this exercise, let the Holy Spirit be your breeze, and list your verses with each letter of T.A.N.D.E.M.

T-Time for Takeoff

_____

_____

_____

_____

_____

A-Alignment

_____

_____

_____

_____

_____

N-Necessary Stops

_____

_____

_____

_____

_____

D-Don't Stop Pedaling

_____

_____

_____

_____

_____

E-Enjoy the Ride

_____

_____

_____

_____

_____

M-Mark the Moment

_____

_____

_____

_____

I hope you enjoyed that assignment. I sure did! It's super exciting for me to apply **all** that we have learned these last twelve weeks to Scripture. This is a key aspect of Riding Tandem with the Lord—learning how He uses **our lives** to tandem personal experiences with the Word to teach us His truth. I just love it!

Here's what I saw in Mary's journey. I see that her preparation for **T-akeoff** happened long before the angel appeared. God saw her heart and knew before the creation of time that she would be highly favored and chosen as the one to carry the Savior into this world. Because of her strong Jewish foundation, Mary knew God personally and **A-ligned** herself to His will without much questioning. I have written in my Bible that the angel got Mary focused on her future assignment, and I'll add A-lignment! I love her honesty, vulnerability, surrender, and gentleness. She was indeed greatly troubled. The word for troubled (Luke 1:29) is *diatarassō*. Sounds like the word distressed to me. I found it interesting that this word meaning to trouble greatly, or to throw into confusion[17] is only used ONCE in the New Testament. It is used to describe Mary's heart. Even afraid, Mary moved forward and surrendered to God's plan. A great lesson for all of us. My favorite depiction of Mary was illustrated by a kindergarten student at our school. The sketch was proportional except for Mary's eyes—they were as big as watermelons! When I saw it, I thought to myself, this picture is right on target! I would have been *diatarassō, too!*

Even afraid, Mary moved forward and surrendered to God's plan.

I also love that God gave her an immediate **N-ecessary Stop.** Knowing the culture of that day, she could have been stoned to death because she was pregnant before marriage. We read that the angel had to tell her to not be afraid and as a confirmation to the endless possibilities of God's power, even her barren cousin, Elizabeth, was pregnant at an old age.[18] Again we see the word **hurry** as Mary went to visit her cousin, Elizabeth, where she was taken care of for three months. Mary **didn't stop pedaling** as she was obedient to being the Lord's servant. She was committed to the ride and stepped into the role of being the Messiah's mother, even though the future was scary and uncertain. Her song in Luke 1:46-56 is her **E-njoying the Ride**. Do you hear the joy?

"My soul glorifies the Lord and my spirit rejoices in God my Savior, for he has been mindful of the humble state of his servant. From now on all generations will call me blessed, for the Mighty One has done great things for me—holy is his name. His mercy extends to those who fear him, from generation to generation." Luke 1:47-50

There are more **M-ark the Moments** than I can count! I am not sure I can choose one in particular. However, I loved that John the Baptist leaped inside of Elizabeth's womb when he "met" Jesus for the first time. I think this is so GOD! He allows us to take joy in the little things and mark them for glory! His glory!

It's really incredible.

We need to **M-ark** the special God-given Moments in our lives. They may be anniversaries, births, weddings, or graduations. They can also be conversations, breakthroughs, fulfilled dreams, and even the moments that aren't so easy. We must have our eyes open to see the Captain leading us through this life. We must have our hearts open to say, "I am the Lord's servant." We can M-ark the Moments and even better—**write them down** as Mary did.

Think of the little moments where God has met you this week. Celebrate this time with Him. Be joyful as you are filled with the promise that He will never leave you. Riding Tandem is a privilege. Lean into His leading, today.

M-ark the special Moments of your Riding Tandem journey with God this week.

_____

_____

_____

_____

_____

_____

_____

_____

_____

_____

_____

_____

_____

Let's continue reading in Luke where we see the shepherd's response to the angels and the birth of Jesus.

Let's begin by reading Luke 2:15-20. (If you want to start from Luke 2:8, you will get a better background for our lesson today.)

What is the similarity between the shepherd's reaction and the Samaritan woman's reaction after they encountered Jesus? (Luke 2:16-17)

_____

_____

_____

What was Mary's reaction to all the events? Why do you think this is significant?

_____

_____

_____

_____

I love when we can connect the Scripture we are reading to other verses we have learned. I believe this is a work of the Holy Spirit. God's Word is alive and touches our hearts in different ways. When we are IN His Word often, we will see connections. They will deepen our faith and enrich our tandem journey!

When both the Samaritan woman and the shepherds encountered Jesus, they felt an urgency to spread the word about their experience. Their personal interaction ignited (stoked) a passion for others to know Christ that still continues to have a ripple effect on our generation. When we read about personal encounters with Jesus in Scripture and heartfelt desires to share these experiences with others, we should be inspired to do the same. These M-ark the Moment times can be the inspiration for someone else's tandem journey to begin.

I lived in Honolulu, Hawaii the summer after my Junior year at SMU and worked at McDonalds. I was on a Campus for Christ Summer Project and our mission was to share the gospel of Jesus in a creative way on the beaches of Waikiki. Not a bad summer—except for the fact that I gave a cute Japanese girl a milk shake instead of a McChicken sandwich due to the language barrier. But my MARK the moment did not happen at Mickey D's nor witnessing on the beach, it happened when I was on my way to the airport to pick up my parents who were coming to visit. There were two girls in the cab with me, and they asked me why I was in Hawaii. My heart just spilled out. It was not forced. It was not something I had to do. No one was watching. I honestly believe it was the first time I shared my love about Jesus in an authentic way. I will have no idea what ripple effect my testimony made on those two girls, but I **treasured** the moment—and marked it. It was the highlight of my whole nine-week experience. It even trumped the advancement from scooping lard into the french fry vat to taking orders at the window. Aloha, Annie.

When was the last time you shared a personal encounter with Jesus with a friend? Did it ignite a passion for that person to want to know Jesus, too?

_____

_____

_____

_____

_____

_____

_____

_____

(* If this is your last small group together, go to page 142 in the journal section to finish Riding Tandem!)

I RIDE
for PRAYER
REQUESTS

1. Let's look at another M-ark the Moment connection from Luke 1:39 and Luke 2:16.

* Read these passages and see if you can find the repeating word.

> "At that time Mary got ready and hurried to a town in the hill country of Judea, ..." LUKE 1:39
>
> "So they hurried off and found Mary and Joseph, and the baby, who was lying in the manger. "
> LUKE 2:16

* What are they hurrying off to do?

I hope you saw the word **hurried**. Riding Tandem has been about leaning into the leading of God, surrendering control, relaxing your grip, and allowing Him to steer at His pace and perfect timing. Now we see the word hurry. What on earth?

I see that both Mary and the shepherds had divine encounters and hurried off to seek the truth about their experiences. Mary hurried to be with Elizabeth and the shepherds hurried off to find the baby. They were **hurrying** to see if God's Word was truth. They both got their answer, too. Mary found Elizabeth was pregnant just as the angel had said, and the shepherds found the baby in a manger swaddled in cloths, just as the angel said. This is the question I ask myself, and you.

* Do we have this hurry conviction to see God's truth at work? How can we get up in the morning with a desire to read Scripture and see where God is going to show up in our day?

Do we hurry to live by the promises of God? Do we hurry to trust Him? If we do, then we will be M-arking this Scripture passage and finding peace in any moment.

2. Let's read Philippians 4:4-9.

* What are all the actions we are to take to hurry to believe in God's promises? I will start us off. I see ten action verbs!

    1. Rejoice.
    2. Rejoice again.
    3. Be gentle and make evident for all to SEE.
    4. _____
    5. _____
    6. _____
    7. _____
    8. _____
    9. _____
    10. _____

* What are the promises from these verses? Again, I will start us off.

    1. The Lord is near.
    2. The peace of God will guard your heart in Jesus.
    3._____
    4. _____

When we **hurry** to see God, there is an urgency to put His promises into practice. Once we do, we will be able to M-ark many special Moments and see Him actively work in our lives. We will encounter the living Christ in a personal way and our stories will have a **ripple effect** for the Kingdom. To often, we hurry to take control, hurry for the next event, and hurry to see things done in our way and in our own timing. Today, let's hurry to see Jesus. Let's open our eyes and see His wonders. Let's tell our story.

Dear Lord, thank You for giving me a story to tell. I pray today I would be in a hurry to study the truth of Your Word, so I can share the story of hope, victory, love, and life. You know everything about me, and I know it's never too late to begin a vibrant relationship with You. You will see me to the mountain tops high, as well as the valleys low. You are my leader, and I will follow You with wholehearted devotion. Thank You for giving us the Bible that continues to inspire us today. Let my story and my testimony be used to invite someone else to Ride Tandem with You. Amen.

3. As we close our study and journaling time together, we are going to look at Luke 2;19.

* What's was Mary's response to all that was happening to her in Luke 2:19?

The word I want us to mark is the word **treasured.** This word is translated from the Greek word "tereo" meaning to guard. Treasured is syn**tereo** meaning to keep safe, to preserve.[19] Mary was M-arking the Moment by **guarding** this special moment in her heart—a moment that marked all history. Mary treasured one of God's richest M-ark the Moments of all history—the birth of Jesus Christ.

I believe we can take this experience and apply it into our lives as well—Our M-ark the Moments. Why? Because we, too, need to **protect Riding Tandem times with God**.

Identify a M-ark the Moment, then identify how you will treasure that moment to keep it safe or to guard it in your heart?

4. Take some time to look up the following Scriptures. What are we to GUARD?

• **Psalm 141:3**

- **Proverbs 4:13, 23**

- **Proverbs 7:2**

- **Luke 12:15**

- **2 Timothy 1:14**

"Through the power of the Holy Spirit who lives within us, carefully guard the precious truth that has been entrusted to you." 1 Timothy 1:14 (NLT)

- **1 John 5:21**

"Dear children, keep away from anything that might take God's place in your hearts." 1 John 5:21 (NLT)

I think this is the perfect way to end our journey together. In order to Ride Tandem, we have to take this relationship with Jesus **seriously**. We have to **treasure** ALL the blessings God has given to us, and we have to **protect** them.

We have to **guard** what we say to one another.
We have to **guard** our hearts and God's teachings.
We have to **guard** against false teachings and all kinds of evil.
We have to **guard** our minds, our souls, and all our ways.
We have to **carefully guard** the PRECIOUS TRUTH that has been entrusted to us.

139

5. How are you going to treasure your journey through Riding Tandem? Have you seen a difference in your walk with Jesus as a result of TANDEM? Share your thoughts.

T-Time for Takeoff

A-Alignment

N-Necessary Stops

D-Don't Stop Pedaling

E-Enjoy the Ride

M-Mark the Moments

Oh, I wish I could see how Riding Tandem has blessed your journey with Jesus!

Let's reflect back right where we started: If we look back to week one, we will see that we received a tandem bicycle with a letter from our Captain. Being that we have studied twelve weeks in Riding Tandem together, I want to see if reading these instructions will put a smile on your face.

Welcome! Let me introduce myself. My name is Captain, and I am overjoyed that you chose Me to ride with you through life. We are going to take amazing adventures together. As your Captain, I know the direction we will be taking. No need to be distracted by all the latest gadgets and gizmos, I have all the equipment you will need. I have plenty of water and be assured, the rest stops are well planned in advance. If you ever feel tired, insecure, or winded, just stop pedaling and coast. I have you in the palm of My hand. If you ever get scared, worried, or doubt My leading, just lean in and trust that I am steering you in the right direction. Make sure to mark the special moments we will have together and always remember to enjoy the ride. Life can get tricky sometimes, but if you trust Me, I will give you eyes to see from My perspective, the right perspective. Do not worry. As your Captain, I am in full control. Before you climb aboard, please read My instructions and know your seating assignment. It is very important to know our takeoff procedures before we ride together on this tandem bicycle.

With everlasting love,
Your Captain

This letter reminds me of reading a brochure before you go on a trip. We won't experience the fullness of the trip unless we experience the journey first hand. Now, we can look back at this instruction manual and say, "Ah, yes. I know **by experience** that my Captain and I will take amazing adventures together. He helps me know when to ride, when to coast, and when to stop altogether. He knows the importance of my T-akeoff procedures, my A-lignment, my N-ecessary Stops, my pressing on through difficulty, my ability to E-njoy the Ride, and my special M-ark the Moments together with Him. All these help me see His glory and hurry to speak about His promises."

NOW IT's YOUR TURN. Write a prayer to Your Captain and thank Him for this journey to Ride Tandem.

I , for one, treasure **you** and the time spent together on this adventure Riding Tandem. My prayer is that we would not forget our journey together. Just as God used the visual of the stars to show Abram how many descendents he would have, we have the visual of the tandem bike to realign us with the purposes God has for us. We have the tandem to remind us to view life from the back seat knowing that God is in control at ALL times. He knows what's ahead and will give us all the strength, endurance, equipment, and patience we need to handle life. We need to stop pedaling at times to coast. We need to keep pedaling at times to run this race with perseverance. We need to remember to enjoy life and mark moments where God shows up. Oh, the glory of knowing Jesus.

Treasure this journey.

Receive the invitation today and enjoy the ride of your life.

I love you dearly.

Annie

Art Project:

Riding Tandem Journal

Art Supplies:

- Composition Notebook
- Template for Riding Tandem Journal
Download at: http://www.thouartexalted.com/
riding-tandem/riding-tandem-journal-template/
- Elmers Glue/ Glue Sticks
- Foam Brush/ Bowl for water
- Colored Fabric
- Scrapbook Paper
- Old Brown Bag
- Scissors
- Buttons, Glitter, Washi Tape
- Twine
- Old Hotel Card/Credit Card

Art Instructions:

1. Open up your composition notebook and lay it's back on the back side of your Brown Bag. Using a pencil, trace around the notebook. Cut out this rectangular form. Using a glue-water mixture (1 part glue/3 parts water), glue it to the outside of your notebook. (See tip on "bubbling.")

2. Take another strip of scrapbook paper (4" x 9.75") and glue a "binder" that covers the front and back. You can also cover the back with Scrapbook paper leaving extra on the front for a binding effect.

3. Download and copy the Journal Template. Cut out the Scripture. Cut shapes and trace them onto your fabric or paper. Plan out where you want the Scripture and shapes and glue them down.

4. Have fun putting the final touches on your Riding Tandem Journal using buttons, sequins, and washi tape (even consider adding flowers to your basket!).

TIPS: • Notebooks: $1 at Dollar Tree • Glue/Water Mixture: 3 parts glue to one part water.
• When gluing paper to notebook, don't use too much glue. If the paper starts to "bubble," use an old credit card or hotel key card to smooth out the paper.

Notes:

1. Definition of wonderful, https://www.blueletterbible.org/lang/lexicon/lexicon.cfm?Strongs=H6381&t=NKJV
2. http://business-finance.blurtit.com/3171446/what-does-duracell-say-about-the-durability-of-their-brand
3. Definition of *watch*: https://www.blueletterbible.org/lang/lexicon/lexicon.cfm?Strongs=G1127&t=KJV
4. Definition of see: http://www.blueletterbible.org/lang/lexicon/lexicon.cfm?Strongs=H1540&t=KJV
5. The Days of Heaven Upon Earth, *Steams in the Desert*, (Grand Rapids, Michigan, Zondervan, Copyright 1925), pg. 198
6. Lauren Daigle, *Trust in You*, Published by Lyrics © Sony/ATV Music Publishing LLC ©2015
7. Definition of *Darak*, https://www.blueletterbible.org/lang/lexicon/lexicon.cfm?Strongs=H1869&t=KJV
8. http://healthyliving.azcentral.com/bicycle-built-two-work-7507.
9. Drive Train: https://en.wikipedia.org/wiki/Chain_drive
10. http://tonyevans.org/mobile/the-confidence-of-faith/
11. Definition of *Kuwn*, https://www.blueletterbible.org/lang/lexicon/lexicon.cfm?Strongs=H3559&t=NIV
12. Definition of *Quwm*, https://www.blueletterbible.org/lang/lexicon/lexicon.cfm?Strongs=H6965&t=NIV
13. Mark Batterson, *Draw the Circle: The 40 Day Prayer Challenge*, (Grand Rapids, Michigan, Zondervan, ©2012), pg. 24
14. Definition of sanctify, www.blueletterbible.org/lang/lexicon/lexicon.cfm?Strongs=H6942&t=NIV
15. J. Danson Smith, *Sit Still*, http://www.cobblestoneroadministry.org/2005_CRM/Poem_SitStillByJDanson-Smith.html
16. Sarah Young, *Jesus Calling*, (Nashville, Tennessee, Thomas Nelson Publishing, ©2004), February 10th, pg. 236
17. Definition of diatarassō, https://www.blueletterbible.org/lang/lexicon/lexicon.cfm?Strongs=G1298&t=NIV
18. http://studybible.info/vines/Trouble%20(Noun%20and%20Verb)
19. Definition of *syntereo*: https://www.blueletterbible.org/lang/lexicon/lexicon.cfm?Strongs=G4933&t=NIV

Annie Pajcic lives in Jacksonville, Florida with her husband and four children. Using her background in youth ministry, art, and graphic design, she started ThouArtExalted in 2007. ThouArtExalted is a non-profit 501(c)(3) ministry inspiring women and girls to live creatively for Christ. When Annie doesn't have paint on her hands, she is writing and designing Bible studies, picking up kids, cooking dinner, or feeding the chickens. Visit her website at **www.thouartexalted.com** for speaking engagements, art ideas, Bible studies, service projects, and devotionals.

SPECIAL THANKS!

I'm so thankful for the study of Riding Tandem. God has taken me through many N-ecessary Stops being a wife and a mom of four (not to mention a few A-lignments!). Jesus is so faithful, and I praise Him for creatively equipping me with His Word. A special thanks to my sweet co-captain, Curry, for his continued encouragement and "way-to-gos!" A BIG SHOUT out to: my amazing board, Joani and Ann, Leah Frye, Sophie Smith, and Brooks Wilder for photography, Heather Stoll for tireless edits, Kevin, Eric, and Mark of CollabCreation film production, and my assistant, sweet Mycah Hunter, for an unending gracious spirit. Thank You, Jesus, for being my Captain and inviting me to ride with You. The journey is thrilling, humbling, and most of all rewarding. Until we see You face to face, let's ride on into eternity. Amen.

James/Following God's Road Signs: One Year Curriculum for Pre-teen/ Teen Girls and Boys

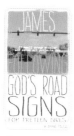

James: Following God's Road Signs is a 27-week Bible study on the book of James for Middle School girls and boys. It is written to encourage and deepen faith when life isn't quite so easy. God is on our side and gives us INSTRUCTIONS for how to navigate—even when we choose to drive our own way. The book of James is a **road map** guiding us in the right direction. *Following God's Road Signs* teaches us to put our FAITH INTO ACTION by stopping, looking at God's map, and asking Him for directions. This study is great for youth groups, small groups, and homeschool groups.

What You Get:

- The book of James verse-by-verse in a fun, creative way
- 27 exciting Bible lessons
- **Creative art projects**
- Dig-deep discussion questions
- Lessons come in a **Digital PDF** format for easy sharing

ARTBox in your INBox: Twelve Month Digital Devotional and Art Projects for Pre-teen/ Teen Girls

ARTBox in Your INBox was developed with pre-teen and teenage girls in mind. ARTBox is a creative devotional lesson that comes directly to your inbox **each month**. This new digital resource offers girls the chance to study God's Word and deepen their relationship with Jesus. ARTBox is also filled with fun art projects, memory verses, recipes, community service ideas, and more!

Each issue of ARTBox in Your INBox offers:

- 12 monthly PDF devotional lessons with real-life application
- FUN and CREATIVE art projects that reinforce Scripture
- Scripture memory verses
- Additional creative activities such as recipes, community service projects, conversation starters, Christian music play lists, and more

He Knows My Name 20/20 Mini Lessons for Girls is a Bible study for middle school girls ages 10-14 based on John 10:3. Jesus is our Good Shepherd and we, His children, are the sheep of His pasture. Using the imagery of sheep and shepherds, He Knows My Name teaches girls that God will always love, protect, and lead into safe pastures. This study also includes five art projects connecting the story of the Good Shepherd into a creative form. Whether used in a personal devotion or a small group setting, the lessons are designed to take about 20 minutes.

What you Get:

- Engaging lesson plans about 20 minutes
- Extra Scripture to dig deeper
- Prayers for each lesson
- Personal application

5 Creative Art Projects

ThouArtExalted APP:
Pre-teen and Teen Girls

ThouArtExalted Ministries APP featuring Awake My Soul Devotionals is a **FREE** devotional app for tween and teen girls to read through the New Testament in ONE YEAR! Each day they will receive a quick devotional right to their phones that will highlight verses from each chapter of the New Testament starting with Matthew. Packed with fun downloadable graphics, journal questions, prayers, and personal applications. Download here: **http://get.theapp.co/998f/**

For Tween and Teen girls
ThouArtExalted Ministries

Visit WWW.THOUARTEXALTED.COM for more information

Made in the USA
Columbia, SC
10 May 2019